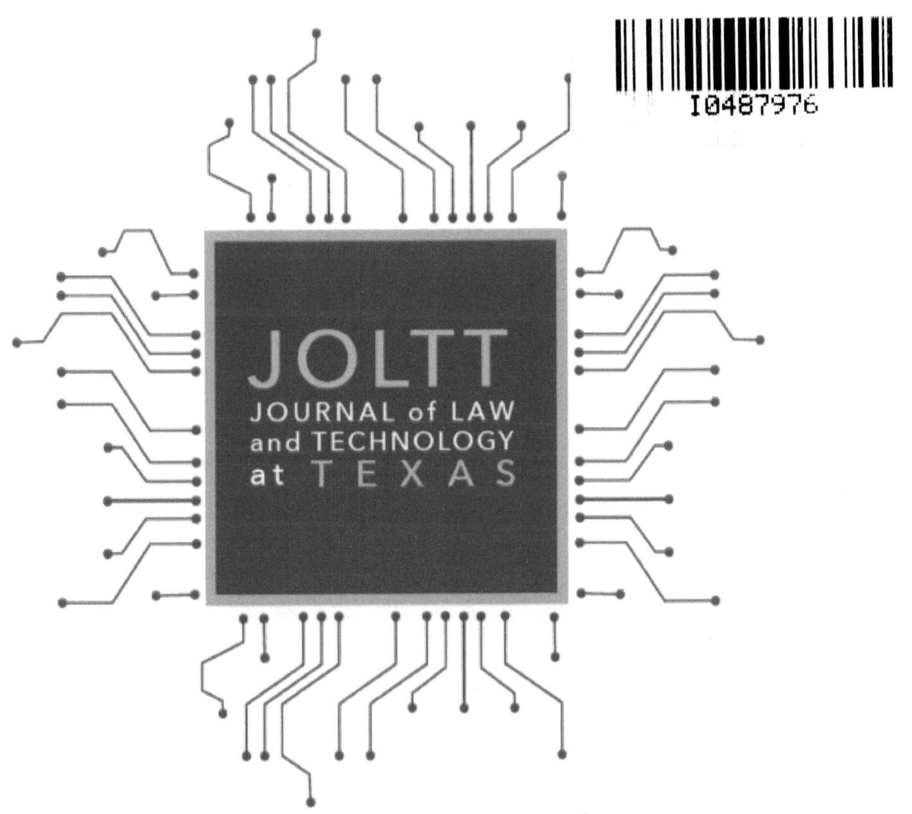

Volume 2

2018-2019

Printed by Lulu Press, Inc., in the United States of America.

ISBN: 978-0-359-34270-9

First printing, 2019.

www.jolttx.com

Masthead

Members of the Editing Staff

ANGLING FOR JUSTICE: USING FEDERAL LAW TO REEL IN CATFISHING
and
DRONES IN CONSTRUCTION

Executive Editors
Daniel Rankin
Elijah Roden

Staff Editors and Contributors
Seth Young
Grace Bowers
Matthew Higgins
Chase Lanfer
Maximillian Shaps
Melanie Froh
Kevin St. George
Marla Hayes
Jacqueline Odom
Daniel Michon
Julie Balogh
Shravan Davuluri
Logan Young
Zhongqi (Zach) Zhao
Austin Lee
Arushi Pandya
Sarah Propst
Aruna Nathan
Jessica Zhang

Online Editors
Tracy Zhang
Hayley Ostrin

Members of the Editing Staff

A New Theory of Fair Use, Re-conceptualized and Updated for Today's Information Society and Press A to Pay: Payment Processing Within Virtual Worlds

Executive Editors

Samuel Higginbotham

Hayley Ostrin

Staff Editors and Contributors

Sarah Hampton Brown

Gabriella Oxford

Laura Lisa Salinas

Danielle Tholen

Brooke Noble

Clara Chalk

Erin Worbs

Zimei Fan

Ritika Gopal

Hunter Baker

James Eastman

Janel Venzant

Myzar Mendoza

Brendon Walsh

Online Editors

Tracy Zhang

Hayley Ostrin

Foreword

In just its third year of existence, the Journal of Law and Technology at Texas (JOLTT) has continued to grow, thanks to the work ethic of our wonderful executive board. Daniel Rankin, JOLTT's Assistant Editor in Chief, has been a powerhouse—designing editing guidelines and managing editors and edits as an Executive Editor. Elijah Roden, our Vice President of Content, also performed beautifully as an Executive Editor, while concurrently helping to organize JOLTT's first Women in Technology Law Panel.[1] Grace Bowers, Vice President of Outreach, led the Women in Technology Law Panel, garnered the support of law firms, and helped perform JOLTT's Technology Lawyer Highlight interviews. Seth Young, Vice President of Membership, managed our members, and has helped put guidelines in place so our members can get the full benefit of belonging to JOLTT. Tracy Zhang, JOLTT's Director of Technology has completely revamped our website, www.jolttx.com, increasing its functionality, readability, and accessibility. This website update is especially important to ensure that JOLTT stays on the forefront of communicating with lawyers in the technology sector.

Special thanks to Founders Alex Sharestani and Clara Chalk, and former Editor in Chief Tyler Oubre, not only for having the vision and grit to bring JOLTT into existence, but for continuing to support JOLTT now that you are both legal practitioners.

Sincerely,

Hayley Ostrin
Editor in Chief
The Journal of Law and Technology at Texas

---

[1] Visit http://jolttx.com/2018/11/26/video-women-in-technology-panel/ to view a recording of this event.

Table of Contents

A New Theory of Fair Use, Re-conceptualized and Updated for Today's Information Society

*Ritika Gopal**

* J.D., 2017, University of Texas School of Law. Thank you, Professor Oren Bracha, for your continued guidance and salient advice over the course of this semester. Working under your supervision during my 3L year was undoubtedly a major highlight of my time at law school. I am far more discerning, thorough, and analytical thanks to you.

TABLE OF CONTENTS

I. INTRODUCTION

Copyright law and the First Amendment's right to free speech are often at conceptual odds with each other. As legal scholar Paul Goldstein puts it: "[C]opyright persists in its potential for conflict with the First Amendment."[1] The former, a government creation, effectuates the idea that ownership of a work is exclusively conferred onto the creator so as to protect her work from unauthorized use by others[2], whereas the latter curtails government restrictions on the people's constitutional right to free speech and expression.[3]

Even so, copyright and free speech are not meant to exist in disharmony. Crucially, the U.S. Constitution contains clauses on *both* copyright and free speech, implying that the Framers intended for copyright to exist within limits. The Constitution's inclusion of both clauses also lends credence to the notion that, within a certain range of conditions, copyright[4] and the First Amendment actually further the same democratic goal: *safeguarding the free and widespread dissemination of expression and ideas.* In search of that point of optimality, several mechanisms have been developed in copyright law that function to balance the preservation of free-speech values with the enforcement of creators' copyright interest in their works.[5] One of those mechanisms is the fair-use doctrine, an affirmative defense in which courts determine whether an unauthorized copy falls under one of several exceptions, such as parody, criticism, or research. It is one of the most unsettled and murkiest areas of the law.[6] As

---

[1] Paul Goldstein, *Copyright and the First Amendment*, 70 COLUM. L. REV. 983, 984 (1970).

[2] U.S. CONST. amend. I.

[3] Copyright law and enforcement draw their persuasive thrust from Article I, § 8, cl. 8 of the U.S. Constitution. It states, in pertinent part, that Congress is empowered to "promote the Progress of Science and useful Arts, by securing for limited Times to Authors and Inventors the exclusive Right to their respective Writings and Discoveries." U.S. CONST. Art. I, § 8, cl. 8.

[4] In other words: The Copyright Clause, which is implemented by the Copyright Act of 1976.

[5] *See* Eldred v. Ashcroft, 537 U.S. 186, 219–221 (2003).

[6] *See* Sony Computer Entertainment America, Inc. 417, 454–55 (1984).

such, this essay specifically focuses on the fair-use doctrine and the extent to which it is effective in harmonizing freedom of expression and copyright.

The way courts apply fair use today is increasingly outmoded. As digital technologies have fundamentally changed the way in which people speak and interact, the fulcrum between freedom of expression and its counterweight, copyright enforcement, has likewise shifted. Today's World Wide Web has made possible the seamless distribution, circulation and exchange of expressive works from person to person, and in turn, the creation of many novel, modern-day channels of expression. In particular, the popularity of collage and appropriation art forms such as mashups and internet "memes" have risen to viral proportions.[7] However, many such collage and appropriation works do not fall within traditional notions of fair use and, as a result, undergo crude judicial analysis. The resulting uncertainty over the reliability of fair use as a balancing tool, then, tends to chill the dissemination of certain types of expression, even though many of these expressions are considered by society as staples of cultural communication in the digital era. Put differently, the overall effect of a shaky fair-use standard is that the shared goal of copyright and the First Amendment strays further away from actualization.

Therefore, the current state of jurisprudential treatment of fair use as a balancing mechanism warrants serious re-examination. Rather than adhering to arcane distinctions, fair use should mirror the *public* normative perception of where the line between speech and copyright exists. As such, this essay proposes and supports the following recommendation for reform: Embracing an expansive, *Cariou*-like conception of fair use that subsumes online-era transformative appropriation/adaptive uses of existing works—in combination with shifting the burden of proof from the fair user to the copyright holder—will reinstate fair use as an effective balancing mechanism between free speech and copyright values. Doing so will realign the fair-use standard not only with today's technological realities, but also with critical democratic theories of expression.

---

[7] *See* Kim Zetter, *Humans Are Just Machines For Propagating Memes*, WIRED (Feb, 29, 2008), https://www.wired.com/2008/02/ted-blackmore/ ("A meme can be a song or snippet of a song, a dance, an urban legend, an expression or behavior, a product brand or even a religion.").

To start, Part II provides background on the relationship between First Amendment and copyright law, as well as why fair use in particular is poised for reform. Part II then explains how digital technologies have fundamentally changed the nature of expression in terms of free speech and copyright. Part III discusses at length the theoretical framework guiding the bulk of this essay's analysis. Part IV delves into the legal landscape of fair use, that is, it provides an analysis of how it is applied in the judicial system. Drawing from that, Part V identifies issues stemming from the application of the fair use standard that, in reality, counters its underlying goal. Based on the analysis in the foregoing sections, Part V lays out a two-part proposal for fair-use reform. Lastly, Part VI provides justifications supporting each part of the proposal.

I. THE SHARED AND DIVERGENT GOALS OF THE FIRST AMENDMENT AND COPYRIGHT

Stated earlier, both the Copyright Clause and Free Speech Clause are housed in the Constitution, implying that the Framers intended for copyright to operate within the confines of the fundamental right to speech. In the most basic terms, the First Amendment protects expression, while copyright law regulates it. Many notable legal scholars have long contended that there is an inherent and, more often than not, problematic tension between the constitutional commitment to protect free speech and the current application of copyright.[8] However, the Supreme Court so far

---

[8] *See* Ned Snow, *Fair Use as a Matter of Law*, 89 DENV. U. L. REV. 1, 32 (2011) ("[T]he copyright tension [with the Free Speech Clause] appears much greater than the fair-use tension [with the Free Speech Clause]: copyright appears to pose a greater threat to free speech than does fair use."); *see also* Ned Snow, *The Forgotten Right of Fair Use*, 62 CASE W. RES. L. REV. 135, 138 (2011) ("At war are speech and copyright."); Abraham Bell & Gideon Parchomovsky, *The Dual-Grant Theory of Fair Use*, 83 U. CHI. L. REV. 1051, 1108 (2016) ("[T]here is some obvious tension between the strategies chosen by free speech law and copyright law to encourage expression . . . It is undeniable that the two bodies of law adopt fundamentally opposite approaches to promoting speech in society."); Rebecca Tushnet, *Copy This Essay: How Fair Use Doctrine Harms Free Speech and How Copying Serves It*, 114 YALE L. J. 535, 540 (2004) (likening copyright to "book burning mandated by law"); Julie Cohen, *Intellectual Privacy and Censorship of the Internet*, 8 SETON HALL CONST L. J. 693, 693 (1998) (labeling copyright a "form of censorship"); Erwin Chemerinsky, *Balancing Copyright Protections and Freedom of Speech: Why the Copyright Extension Act is Unconstitutional*, 36 LOY. L.A. L. REV. 83, 95 (2003) (asserting that "the Copyright Term Extension Act should be deemed to fail intermediate scrutiny and thus to violate the First Amendment.").

has consistently rejected any notion that copyright and the First Amendment are in tension or are incompatible in their current form; rather, the Court insists they are complimentary.[9] The way the Court sees it, copyright incentivizes the creation and dissemination of published expression, while the First Amendment restrains the government from limiting it.[10] Though, this view can easily be framed in the negative: "*Copyright represents a government restraint* on the public's ability to communicate copied expression [by] restrain[ing] those who speak expression already articulated by another," while "free speech condemns [that very restraint]."[11]

Therefore, in light of the growing rift between the judicial sentiment espoused in *Eldred* and the technological paradigm shift in expressive activity, a critical choice must be made at this juncture: either accept the Supreme Court's assertion regarding the harmonious nature of the relationship between copyright and speech and move on, or challenge that notion and come up with ways to reform features of copyright such that they remain functionally effective, even when the surrounding circumstances change. This essay is decidedly an assertion of the latter. Indeed, as copyright scholar Melville Nimmer asserts, free speech is about self-expression.[12] If the goal of the Copyright Clause in the Constitution is "[t]o promote the Progress of Science and useful Arts, by securing for limited Times to Authors and Inventors the exclusive Right to their respective Writings and Discoveries,"[13] then it would seem that the Copyright Act's policy balance—between incentivizing the production of

---

[9] *See* Eldred v. Ashcroft, 537 U.S. 186, 219 (2003) ("[C]opyright's limited monopolies are compatible with free speech principles. Indeed, copyright's purpose is to *promote* the creation and publication of free expression.").

[10] *Id.* (emphasis added).

[11] Ned Snow, *The Forgotten Right of Fair Use*, 62 CASE W. RES. L. REV. 135, 138 (2011).

[12] Melville B. Nimmer, *Does Copyright Abridge the First Amendment Guarantees of Free Speech and Press?*, 17 UCLA L. REV. 1180 (1970).

[13] U.S. CONST. Art. I, sec. 8, cl. 8.

creative works and safeguarding public access to those works—must effectuate the Copyright Clause's expression-protective goal.[14]

In other words, the main objective of copyright exclusivity is to maximize the dissemination of creative and expressive works. Therefore, if the public perception of what is expressive has shifted, or if the means of accomplishing self-expression has fundamentally changed due to disruption brought by technological development, then it is worth exploring whether certain aspects of copyright law should be reformed in order to ensure that the underlying policy of both the Copyright Clause and First Amendment is fulfilled in today's contexts.

Accordingly, this essay operates under the assumption that copyright and the right to free speech were meant to further the same democratic goal: *safeguarding the free and widespread dissemination of expression and ideas.* The starting point for reform, then, is to explore ways to reunify copyright and free speech such that they indeed work towards their shared goal—even in the digital age. Specifically, this requires examining the area in which copyright and free speech intersect. Embedded within copyright law are legal mechanisms that function to safeguard free-speech principles. These mechanisms include the widely accepted idea/expression dichotomy;[13] the first-sale doctrine;[14] the limited term of a copyright;[15] and the fair-use standard.[16] However, not all of these mechanisms are created equal in terms of their amenability for reform. As law professor Michael J. Madison writes:

> The idea/expression distinction is almost impossibly elusive; licensing of digital content presses the first sale doctrine nearly to the breaking point; and in *Eldred v. Ashcroft* the Supreme Court determined that Congress has nearly unlimited discretion in setting copyright's

[14] Nicolas Suzor, *Access, Progress, and Fairness: Rethinking Exclusivity in Copyright*, 15(2) VAND. J. ENT. & TECH. L. 294, 322 (2008); U.S.C. § 102(b) ("In no case does copyright protection for an original work of authorship extend to any idea, procedure, process, system, method of operation, concept, principle, or discovery, regardless of the form in which it is described, explained, illustrated, or embodied in such work.").

[15] U.S.C. § 109 (where a buyer of a copyrighted work may do what he may with the work as long as it does not infringe upon the exclusive rights of the work's copyright owner); *see supra* note 3; U.S.C. § 107.

> duration. Fair use appears to be the battleground state of copyright politics. To paraphrase Lloyd Weinreb, fair use embodies the true meaning of copyright—whatever that is.[16]

Therefore, fair use is the chosen object of analysis in this essay, since it appears to promise a greater return on investment (i.e., implemented reform) as compared to the other copyright-free speech-balancing mechanisms.

Indeed, fair use is uniquely flexible, "which is particularly important with regard to copyright laws, because they must be constantly adjusted to face the changing needs of rapidly developing technology. [Such] [f]lexibility . . . is necessary for achieving the goals of copyright laws in such a dynamic environment, and for securing breathing space for its creators."[17] The fair-use doctrine operates as an affirmative defense in copyright-infringement lawsuits. When a defendant is accused of copyright infringement, she can assert in court that her use of the copyrighted material in question constitutes fair use. Judges will then assess whether the facts and circumstances surrounding the alleged infringement support a finding of fair use. The outcome of fair-use disputes, however, is typically hard to predict, as fair-use determinations are fact-intensive, and the judge enjoys a wide breadth of discretion when making such determinations.

The flexibility of fair use arises from its four factors. The four fair-use factors judges consider are as follows: (1) purpose and character of the use, including whether such use is of a commercial nature and/or is transformative; (2) nature of the copyrighted work; (3) the amount and substantiality of the portion used in relation to the copyrighted work as a whole; and (4) the effect of the use upon the potential market.[18] The first factor is particularly important, as it generally accounts for a larger portion

---

[16] Michael J. Madison, *Rewriting Fair Use and the Future of Copyright Reform*, 23 CARDOZO ART & ENT. L. J. 391, 393 (2005) [*hereinafter Rewriting Fair Use*].

[17] Niva Elkin-Koren & Orit Fischman-Afori, *Rulifying Fair Use*, 59 ARIZ. L. REV. 161, 162 (2017).

[18] Campbell v. Acuff-Rose Music, 510 U.S. 569 (1994).

of the judicial imagination relative to the other three factors.[19] Indeed, in *Campbell v. Acuff-Rose Music*, the Supreme Court held that "transformative" uses—uses that add new material in a manner that reflects critically on the original copyrighted work—are favored and assumed to be less likely to damage the copyright owner's market interests.[20] Such uses are considered objectively valuable to culture and society at large and are therefore prioritized over one's copyright interest in the original work.

By virtue of the four factors in fair use, there is room for malleability without uprooting the foundations of copyright law. Specifically, evaluating what exactly renders a given use of copyrighted material "transformative" under the first fair-use factor, so as to bring it outside the classification of "derivative" work (an integral part of a copyright holder's set of exclusive rights), is a viable, albeit challenging, path of inquiry.[21] Indeed, in a culture characterized by interactivity and mass participation online, people are able to piece together and continuously distribute, circulate, and exchange bits of culture from person to person quickly and cheaply. Some argue that now-popular contemporary appropriation art poses a special free-speech problem.[22] Collage and appropriation works of expression—or as law professor Jack M. Balkin describes it, "the creative and opportunistic use of trademarks, cultural icons, and bits of media products to create, innovate, re-edit, alter, and form pastiches and collage"—are a standard technique of speech and expression

---

[19] *See id.* at 569; *see also* Cariou v. Prince, 714 F.3d 694, 705 (2d Cir. 2013) ("The first statutory factor to consider, which addresses the manner in which the copied work is used, is "[t]he heart of the first use inquiry") (quoting Blanch v. Koons, 467 F.3d 244, 251 (2d Cir. 2006)).

[20] *See Campbell*, 510 U.S. at 579 ("The central purpose of this investigation is to see . . . whether the new work merely 'supersede[s] the objects' of the original creation, or instead adds something new, with a further purpose or different character, altering the first with new expression, meaning, or message; it asks, in other words, whether and to what extent the new work is 'transformative.'") (internal citations omitted).

[21] Rebecca Tushnet, *Copy This Essay: How Fair Use Doctrine Harms Free Speech and How Copying Serves It*, 114 YALE L. J. 535, 544 ("The derivative works right is difficult to reconcile with a transformation-friendly fair use.") [hereinafter Tushnet].

[22] *See* Sean M. O'Conner, *The Internet Does Not Reset the Copyright-Free Speech Balance*, Center For The Protection of Intellectual Property (November 2013), at 4 [hereinafter O'Conner].

in the digital world.[23] At the heart of today's fair-use debate, then, is determining which "uses" of copyrighted material should be considered acceptable, that is, which "uses" should be considered objectively valuable enough to democratic culture such that they warrant protection under "transformative" fair use.

As of now, the fair-use standard in its current form is, in Professor Jessica Litman's words, "a troublesome safe harbor for First Amendment rights."[24] Thus, fair use—though "spectacularly unsuccessful" as applied—is in dire need of reexamination.[25] Therefore, the starting point for analysis in this essay will be to evaluate the criteria of what makes a work "transformative" against the backdrop of change in expression and culture brought on by the digital revolution.

III. An Overview Of Today's Technological Realities With Respect To New Modes of Expression

The digital revolution has recast the system of free expression in a new light: It has enabled widespread cultural participation and interaction that previously could not exist on the same scale.[26] For example, the advent of the internet and attendant technologies (e.g., the MP3 file format, peer-to-peer file-sharing networks, social media networks) has dramatically lowered the cost of copying and distributing content. It has also made it easier for individuals to innovate with existing content, comment on it, and build upon it. Now, finding themselves in the thick of digital communication that is characterized by seamless interactivity and mass participation, consumers of content are able to "copy, modify, annotate, collate, transmit, and distribute [it] by storing it in digital form."[27] In other

---

[23] Jack M. Balkin, *Digital Speech and Democratic Culture: A Theory of Freedom of Expression for the Information Society*, 79 N.Y.U. L. REV. 1, 11 (2004) [hereinafter *Digital Speech and Democratic Culture*].

[24] Jessica Litman, *Reforming Information Law in Copyright's Image*, 22 DAYTON L. REV. 587, 612 (1997).

[25] *See id.*

[26] Balkin, *supra* note 23, at 2.

[27] Balkin, *supra* note 23, at 2.

words, people can, with relative ease, combine and mix content with other existing content to produce something entirely new as a means of expressing themselves to the world.

Speech and expression have become "democratized because technologies of distribution and transmission are put in the hands of an increasing number of people and increasingly diverse segments of society throughout the planet . . . In the digital age, distribution and innovation go hand in hand."[28] The mass popularity and distribution of cross-genre artist mash-ups[29] are a prime illustration of this phenomenon:

> [T]he mash-up is a response to larger technological, institutional, and social contexts. Through themes of irony, empowerment, and re-appropriation, the mash-up serves as a fitting expression of today's youth media experience . . . Mashers rewrite the pop canon . . . and subvert taste hierarchies that dominate pop music . . . Their deconstructionist, re-appropriationist mentality—whereby texts are stripped of original meaning and soldered to others—also blurs the high-low culture divide.[30]

Indeed, emerging communications technologies have given life to new modes of critical and cultural expression, some of which encompass forms of collage and appropriation art that thrive online—e.g., remixes, mash-ups, sonic sampling, memes, and many more. Of crucial importance is the fact that many of these types of works can arguably be considered culturally valuable, as their contribution to the diversity of expression and speech is certainly notable. Some such works can be considered heterodox and are especially valuable to society, in that they "challenge broadly held views, beliefs or tastes, and include content that is outside the mainstream,

---

[28] Balkin, *supra* note 23, at 8–9.

[29] A mash-up is a sound recording that is comprised of samples taken from other recordings and remixed to create a single new track.

[30] Michael Serazio, *The Apolitical Irony of Generation Mash-Up: A Cultural Case Study in Popular Music*, 31 Popular Music and Society 79, 79–91 (2008) [hereinafter *The Apolitical Irony of Generation Mash-Up*].

is avant-garde, or is aimed at preferences and tastes that are relatively marginal."[31] Indeed, some music historians frame the loosening of production boundaries (as seen in mash-up culture) as an expression of empowerment and resistance against mainstream perceptions of music.[32] At a minimum, such digital art forms play a significant role in changing the public's relationship to music.[34]

Yet, the proliferation of digital technologies has opened up new opportunities for rights-holders to aggressively limit and control maverick means of cultural participation and interaction, rendering the underlying tension between copyright and freedom of speech much more pronounced. In addition, copyright law has developed and been legislated in a way that skews incentives and rewards for the content industry against public access to copyrighted works.[33] Armed with advanced online technologies, copyright holders receive notice of individuals' unauthorized use of their works and are able to track individuals' copying activities. Unsurprisingly, rights-holders frequently leverage the threat of litigation against the public to maintain control over access to their works.[34] At the same time, they consistently reject complaints that their "digital rights management schemes inhibit freedom of expression because they eliminate fair use and

---

[31] *See* Oren Bracha & Talha Syed, *Beyond Efficiency: Consequence-Sensitive Theories of Copyright*, 29 BERKELEY TECH. L. J. 229, 269 (2014) [hereinafter *Beyond Efficiency*].

[32] *See* Serazio, *The Apolitical Irony of Generation Mash-Up*, at 85.

[33] Nicolas Suzor, Access, Progress, and Fairness: Rethinking Exclusivity in Copyright, 15(2) VAND. J. ENT. & TECH. L. 294, 324 (2008) (copyright as applied today supports an "asymmetry in market power between professional artists and publisher intermediaries and generally fails to adequately reward all but superstar artists . . . [I]t provides extremely high rewards to an extremely small proportion of creators who are able to win a lottery for attention.").

[34] *See* Kerry Sheehan & Kit Walsh, "BWP Media v. Polyvore: It's All About Control", *Elec. Frontier Found.*, Feb. 22, 2017, *available at* https://www.eff.org/deeplinks/2017/02/bwp-media-v-polyvore-its-all-about-control ("Big media gatekeepers have a long history of trying to use copyright law to maintain control of technology that enables ordinary people to take popular culture into their own hands. In the 1980's it was home video recording, in the 2000's, remote video storage. Since then, the battle has been waged over various forms of user-generated content platforms and search tools.").

shrink the public domain."[35] However, in the process of aggressively asserting their rights online and relying on the current interpretation of fair use, they often fail to distinguish fair users from infringers.[36]

It follows, then, that emerging technologies have weakened the reliability of fair use as a balancing mechanism between copyright and free expression. This has resulted in a sweeping conflation of all types of infringement in legal thinking. For example, judges often lump together certain instances of "*transformative appropriation* (e.g., when a rap artist samples a song without permission) with *plagiarism* (e.g., copying a Beethoven symphony and claiming it as one's own) and *music piracy* (e.g., burning a compact disc and sharing it with thousands of other network users).[37] Of course, this is not surprising because the underlying message of collaged and appropriation works is largely premised on their usage and referencing of other creative works. To the extent that someone needs to use or reference a copyrighted work to express a markedly different point, or to comment on or parody the work, the Supreme Court's current position is that the fair-use mechanism codified in the Copyright Act provides an effective means to do so.[38] Yet this position largely underestimates the changes brought on by technology.[39]

---

[35] *Id.* at 22.

[36] *See* Ned Snow, *Proving Fair Use: Burden of Proof as Burden of Speech*, 31 CARDOZO L. REV. 1781, 1805 (2010) ("From the standpoint of the copyright holders, these suits seem necessary to protect their rights: The larger Internet audience creates a greater potential for individual web posters to cause excessive damage to copyright value. But, in bringing suits against individuals, copyright holders often fail to discriminate between infringers and fair users.") [hereinafter *Proving Fair Use*].

[37] Joanna Dembers, *Steal This Music: How Intellectual Property Law Affects Creativity*, Athens: U of Georgia, 119 (2006) [hereinafter Dembers].

[38] *See id.*

[39] *See* Lawrence B. Solum, *The Future of Copyright: Free Culture: How Big Media Uses Technology and the Law to Lock Down Culture and Control Creativity*, 83 TEXAS L. REV. 1137, 1138 (2005) (reviewing Lawrence Lessig, *Free Culture: How Big Media Uses Technology and the Law to Lock Down Culture and Control Creativity* (2004)) (pointing out that Legal scholar Joseph P. Liu has proposed that the scope of fair use should grow over time to subsume benign uses of copyrighted works); *see also* Lawrence Lessig, *Code and Other Laws of Cyberspace* (New York: Basic Books, 1999) at 124 ("Should the architecture [of the digital technologies] allow perfect control over intellectual property, or

Herein lies the major problem with copyright enforcement today: Despite the emergence of new and culturally valuable forms of art on the internet, many such creative works are considered to violate copyright because they fall outside many courts' stiff perception of what constitutes a "transformative" fair use. In reality, the culture of sharing expressive works online is too protean and multifaceted for the current fair-use standard to successfully delineate some uses as good and fair (e.g., sampling in hip-hop, a key ingredient of the genre) from those that are objectively bad (e.g., commercial piracy). Fair use, in theory, should be conceptually malleable, so that it is able to continually calibrate its policy calculus with widely accepted cultural norms about expression and expressive activity. The justification for the manner in which the "safety valve" between infringement and protected expression is administered should be grounded in public norms surrounding expressive activity. Yet collage and appropriation artists increasingly face threats of litigation or are outright charged with copyright infringement, despite the fact that such art forms are increasingly viewed by today's information society as a valuable form of expression and speech. Put simply, the existing rift between digital communication technologies and copyright enforcement—manifested in courts' application of fair use—impermissibly starves freedom of expression online and the critical democratic underpinnings of copyright.

IV. Chosen Parameters of Analysis

In order to assess the extent to which fair use, in its current form, successfully balances free-speech values with copyright interests in the context of the digital revolution, a framework for analysis must be determined at the outset. Therefore, the following discussion on fair use as it applies to digital-era expressive works will be structured around certain chosen parameters.

First, the scope of this essay is limited to a specific subset of fair-use materials. The analysis will focus on modern-day appropriation and collage works, which constitute a relatively narrow sliver of works typically known to trigger inquiry into fair use. As stated earlier, such works are increasingly pervading mass communications among today's information society. Indeed, many argue that contemporary appropriation

---

should we build into the architecture an incompleteness that guarantees a certain aspect of public use? Or a certain space for individual freedom?").

art presents a unique free-speech problem.[40] This is because "modern self-expression often uses the content of others as a cultural touchstone identity or to ground expression in a certain context," yet is largely unprotected by fair use.[41] The emergence of such a problem is perhaps unsurprising, since the abundance and diversity in creative expression—largely precipitated by the rapid rise and development of the internet—have significantly altered social norms (i.e., "copynorms") regarding the legal issues that stem from the use of copyrighted material.[42] To provide a well-known example, the emergence of the MP3 file format was a turning point in copyright-infringement history. It led to an era where unauthorized copying, alteration, and sharing of music files—whether that be in the form of MP3s attached to emails, torrents on file-sharing networks, or uploads of user-generated remixes onto social media platforms—became a widely accepted norm.[43]

Another seminal example, of course, is the proliferation of online memes as a large-scale expressive activity. Interestingly, the ubiquity of memes online is quite democratic in nature; it constitutes a "cultural evolution and the shaping of the self through cultural exchange on the other . . . [where] everyone gets to participate in the distribution and dissemination of memes, which are the building blocks of cultural software that constitutes individuals as individuals."[44] Within the memetic space of expression is where copyright law truly struggles. For example, in 2016, Getty Images pursued multiple infringement cases against a host of blogs for posting the "Socially Awkward Penguin" meme, a well-known darling of internet meme culture, alleging that the images used violate Getty

---

[40] *See* O'Conner, *supra* note 22, at 4.

[41] *See* O'Conner, *supra* note 22, at 2.

[42] Mark F. Schultz, Copynorms: Copyright Law and Social Norms, *Intellectual Property and Information Wealth* (Peter Yu ed., forthcoming), available at BERKELEY CTR. FOR L. & TECH., 2006, Paper 26, at 1, http://repositories.cdlib.org/bclt.Its/26.

[43] ALEX S. CUMMINGS, DEMOCRACY OF SOUND 81 (2013).

[44] Balkin, *supra* note 23, at 37, n. 65.

Images' right to create derivative works based upon its copyrighted work.[45] Had the targeted blog decided not to settle, it would most likely have argued that the meme is a "transformative" fair use. In such scenarios, the fair-use distinction between "derivative" and "transformative" is demonstrably difficult to apply. One must ask, then, what does copyright protection mean in an age characterized by an abundance of online creative expression, collaging, and file-sharing? Therefore, whether fair use needs to be recalibrated to such modern-day, appropriative uses of copyrighted material is certainly worth exploring.

Second, the analysis of fair use and subsequent recommendations for reform must be anchored in established theories of expression that apply to speech and copyright. Importantly, the chosen theories of speech and copyright must be ones that complement and support each other doctrinally. Accordingly, this essay will apply a hybrid theory of free expression that interweaves the "Millian" theory of free speech with consequence-sensitive democratic theories of copyright, specifically self-determination and cultural democracy. The reason free-speech theory and democratic theories of copyright are able to be linked, at a broad level, is that both operate on the assumption that there is freedom of expression at both the individual and collective cultural level, which only occurs in an environment where the critical conditions for meaningful free choice and equal access to participate in collective expression are continually nurtured. Moreover, these theories can be linked because both the First Amendment and copyright laws are inspired by the same goal: safeguarding the free and widespread dissemination of expression and ideas.

a. Free speech theory

Philosopher John Stuart Mill's theory of speech was based on the idea that free speech is a necessary means toward fostering a robust "marketplace of ideas"—that, regardless of the degree of veracity in dissenting concerns, exposure to *all* ideas aides in the societal search for truth.[46] Midway through his seminal work *On Liberty*, Mill expanded on

---

[45] Caitlin Dewey, *How copyright is killing your favorite memes*, THE WASH. POST (Sept. 8, 2015), https://www.washingtonpost.com/news/the-intersect/wp/2015/09/08/how-copyright-is-killing-your-favorite-memes/?noredirect=on&utm_term=.32793847c05f.

[46] Irene M. Ten Cate, *Speech, Truth, and Freedom: An Examination of John Stuart Mill's and Justice Oliver Wendell Holmes's Free Speech Defenses*, 22 YALE J. of L. & HUMAN. 36, 38 (2013) [hereinafter Cate].

his arguments for broad freedom of expression.[47] He asserted that society should not merely tolerate, but embrace objectionable speech, for four reasons: First, nobody is infallible, and therefore people should be open to the possibility that an opinion diverging from the mainstream may be true; second, an opinion, while generally erroneous, may contain an ounce of truth that is missing from the mainstream opinion; third, even if the mainstream opinion accounts for the complete truth, those who harbor the opinion will remain unaware of the grounds and rationale supporting the opinion if it is not frequently challenged; fourth, without public discourse and debate, "the meaning of the [opinion] itself will be in danger of being lost, or enfeebled, and deprived of its vital effect on the character and conduct."[48] According to Mill, freedom of speech—and in turn, wide latitude in expression—fosters authenticity, genius, individuality, and human flourishing.[49]

This essay therefore operates on the assumption that the conditions articulated by Mill are part of the desired goal of the right to free speech and copyright. Indeed, much of First Amendment jurisprudence has been grounded in Mill's theory. The "marketplace of ideas" rationale, in particular, has appeared in key free-speech cases such as *Abrams v. United*

---

[47] *Id.* at 38.

[48] *Id.*; John Stuart Mill, *On Liberty*, *reprinted in* On Liberty And Other Essays 21 (John Gray ed., 1998) (1859) ("[T]he peculiar evil of silencing the expression of an opinion, is, that it is robbing the human race; posterity as well as the existing generation; those who dissent from the opinion, still more than those who hold it. If the opinion is right, they are deprived of the opportunity of exchanging error for truth: if wrong, they lose, what is almost as great a benefit, the clearer perception and livelier impression of truth, produced by its collision with error.").

[49] *See* Cate, *supra* note 46.

States,[50] *United States v. Rumely*,[51] and *Brandenburg v. Ohio*.[52] Essentially, the main thrust behind Mill's theory is that if certain types of speech are banned, people will not be able to benefit from the silenced opinion that may be true. Nor will they be able to make meaningful and critical choices when it comes to constructing an informed worldview. Applied to the realm of copyright, perhaps the same can be said for the current application of fair use and how it silences certain Internet-era forms of expression and any "truth" that may be imbued within them.

b. Democratic theories of copyright: self-determination & cultural democracy

Linked to Mill's formulation of free speech are certain democratic theories of copyright that are equally relevant to the fair-use doctrine. The two democratic theories of copyright chosen for this essay are self-determination and cultural democracy. These theories are distinct from traditional rights-based justifications of copyright because they are primarily concerned with the broader societal *consequences* generated by a specific rule on enforcing copyright.[53]

The self-determination theory of copyright, or the idea that free expression is a necessary component of individual self-determination, refers to the "ability of individuals to reflectively form and revise their own

---

[50] 250 U.S. 616, 630 (1919) (Holmes, J., dissenting) ("[W]hen men have realized that time has upset many fighting faiths, they may come to believe even more than they believe the very foundations of their own conduct that the ultimate good desired is better reached by *free trade in ideas*—that the best test of truth is the power of the thought to get itself accepted in the competition of the market, and that truth is the only ground upon which their wishes safely can be carried out. That at any rate is the theory of our Constitution. It is an experiment, as all life is an experiment.") (emphasis added).

[51] 345 U.S. 41, 56 (1953) (Douglas, J., concurring) ("Like the publishers of newspapers, magazines, or books, this publisher bids for the minds of men in the market place of ideas.").

[52] 395 U.S. 444 (1969) (restating the modern high standard that call-to-action speech must meet before being prohibited by the First Amendment).

[53] *See* Bracha & Syed, *supra* note 31, at 245–46.

conception of good, and effectively pursue a life plan for realizing it."[54] In the words of legal scholars Oren Bracha and Talha Syed:

> The ultimate value in self-determination resides in persons' ends being truly their own, meaning reflectively adopted, chosen, and refined by themselves, determining their projects and preferences free from both coercion and manipulation. This entails taking seriously the idea of free choice and the conditions it requires . . . I[ing] a meaningful array of options from which to choose, the capacity to understand and evaluate the options, and the opportunity and means to critically reflect upon and possibly revise one's choices and sense of attractive alternatives.[56]

Applied to freedom of speech, expression as a communicative activity is integral to the critical conditions of genuine free choice as well as the formation of individuals' broader worldviews. *Free* expression is the means by which individuals form meaningful preferences, as it "exposes [them] to competing options, allows them to articulate their own views and subject them to critical evaluation by others . . . [and] supplies the process through which people compare, reflect, and revise their choices."[55] Indeed, individual choices (along with individuals' preferences revealed by them) through expressive activity are truly autonomous and self-determinative "*only* to the extent that the conditions exist for reflective, discerning choices among a meaningful array of alternatives."[56]

Therefore, aggressive control exercised by rights-holders via copyright mechanisms (like fair use) over the degree of diversity in options and individuals' access to and usage of expressive content seriously frustrates the process by which they form their preferences and exercise

---

[54] *Id.* at 251.

[56] *Id.*

[55] *Id.* at 252.

[56] *Id.* at 263 (emphasis added).

autonomy and self-determination.[57] To put it in Millian terms, meaningful self-determination can only occur in an environment (i.e., a "marketplace of ideas") that is devoid of such control and manipulation by others and instead creates opportunities for critical reflection and revision of one's views. Self-determination, in other words, prizes genuine free choice under ideal conditions[58] over *maximum* choice, in which objectively mainstream options dominate the range and selection of choices. Put simply, wide latitude in choice over expressive activity—even where some expressive works are quantitatively less desired by the majority than the competing mainstream options—is a necessary condition for genuine free choice and individual self-determination.[59]

Cultural democracy as theory of copyright is a logical outgrowth of political-democracy theories, which deal with implementing the concept of individual self-determination at the societal level. Political-democracy theories are specifically concerned with decisions occurring in the political sphere that are "inherently collective or irreducibly social in nature."[60] The idea behind these theories is that fulfilling individual self-determination, within the context of such decisions, requires having in place procedures for collective decision-making that both reflect and facilitate the individual autonomy of all members of society.[61] Importantly, political-democracy theories of expression import a key premise of the self-determination

---

[57] *See id.*; *see also* Neil Netanel, *Copyright's Paradox* 19 (2008); Elkin-Koren, *Cyberlaw and Social Change: A Democratic Approach to Copyright Law in Cyberspace*, 14 CARDOZO ARTS & ENT. L.J. 215, 224–32 (1996) [hereinafter *Cyberlaw and Social Change*].

[58] Where ideal conditions are when an individual can choose from a robust marketplace of ideas and options and has the ability to critically understand and reflect upon the differences among options as well as revise and add to his worldview.

[59] *See* Bracha & Syed, *supra* note 31, at 262 ("[A] high normative premium is placed on critical expression due to its role in encouraging critical reflection on, and presenting alternatives to, existing options, especially those that are dominant or widely held. Moreover, ensuring steady exposure to such expression is also likely to cultivate the faculties needed to exercise meaningful reflective choice, since '[t]he mental and moral, like the muscular powers, are improved only by being used.'") (citing JOHN STUART MILL, ON LIBERTY 55 (Batoche Books 2001) (1859)).

[60] *Id.* at 253.

[61] *Id.*

theory of expression, that the critical conditions of free choice at the individual level are necessary for genuine free choice at the collective level.[62] For example, public access to a meaningful array of competing options from which to choose is necessary for genuine free choice at the collective level.

Accordingly, these decision-making processes that give effect to political self-determination at the collective level must fulfill the following two requirements: (1) They must ensure that the higher-order, critical conditions arising in the context of *individual* self-determination apply in equal measure to political *collective* self-determination, and (2) they must ensure that the input of all individuals is given equivalent weight and that each individual enjoys equal opportunity to participate by providing that input.[63] Put differently, through freedom in expressive activity, individuals can assess alternative views and choices and evaluate competing options. And, when extended into the public sphere through collective decision-making processes, expressive activity—when free, diverse, and open—enables individuals to exercise individual self-determination in the form of civic agency, which is key to maintaining a political democracy.[64]

Cultural democracy theory takes a further step with respect to individual and collective self-determination. It extends concepts of free choice within political democracy into the wider cultural sphere, where arguments supporting self-determination in the context of political democracy may run dry. Much like with political democracy, culture in this theory refers to the "irreducibly interactive or social processes through which meanings are forged, communicated, enacted, interpreted, adapted, challenged, revised, recombined and so forth."[65] Cultural democracy as a theory of expression is grounded in the assumption that individuals are

[62] *Id.*

[63] *See id.*

[64] *See id.* ("Participation in the public sphere is also where individuals develop the skills and habits of self- determination necessary for agency as a citizen, including the propensity to seek information, capacities of critical discernment and reflection, and the ability to articulate and communicate one's own views.").

[65] Bracha & Syed, *supra* note 31, at 255.

"deeply socially situated selves"[66] interacting within a wider social and cultural matrix, which legal scholar William Fisher refers to as "[t]he increasingly dense cloud of images, sounds, and symbols through which we move."[67] Indeed, the idea of democratic culture encapsulates the inherent duality of freedom of expression. Freedom of expression is deeply individual, yet it is in equal measure deeply collective because it is deeply cultural. Individuals exercise this freedom in the aggregate by participating in this speech–culture system: "[They] interact with each other, agree and disagree, gossip and shame, criticize and parody, imitate and innovate, support and praise . . . [They] make new meanings and new ideas out of old ones."[68]

What is key to this theory, then, is ensuring that people's freedom of expression in the cultural realm is *collectively meaningful*. Therefore, cultural democracy requires that principles of individual and collective self-determination apply with equal force within the cultural realm. And, going beyond cultural self-determination, cultural democracy theory requires that individuals be afforded equal access and the capacity to actively engage with culture—i.e., "to develop, change, and subvert it."[69] Therefore, the same two requirements for collective decision-making processes in political democracies are equally salient here: (1) Individuals must possess genuine free choice, meaning that the critical conditions that foster, for example, an individual's ability to meaningfully evaluate an option from a diverse set of competing options must be safeguarded; and (2) meaning-making power must be decentralized and individuals must be given equal opportunity to effectively participate in shaping their own subjective tastes within the vast cultural matrix of symbolic and expressive material. In simpler terms, cultural democratic theory of expression is distinguished from the rest by its deep commitment to decentralize meaning-making and enable all individuals to *meaningfully* participate in shaping culture.

---

[66] *See id.* at 254.

[67] WILLIAM FISHER, PROMISE TO KEEP: TECHNOLOGY, LAW AND THE FUTURE OF ENTERTAINMENT 30 (2004).

[68] Balkin, *supra* note 23, at 4–5 (cleaned up).

[69] Bracha & Syed, *supra* note 31, at 255.

c. Combined: a democratic theory of critical expression vis-à-vis free speech and copyright

Taken together, the self-determination and cultural democratic theories of expression emphasize safeguarding: (1) the higher-order conditions that are critical to individuals' genuine choice, that is, their ability to understand, reflect upon, and evaluate a meaningful range of competing options; and (2) the ability for all to engage on equal terms in such expressive activity at the collective, cultural level. An environment that reflects such conditions is democratically "valuable because it gives ordinary people a fair opportunity to participate in the creation and evolution of the processes of meaning-making that shape them and become part of them."[70]

These critical conditions are integral to the aims of the Free Speech Clause and Copyright Clause, whose goal is to safeguard the free and widespread dissemination of expression and ideas. Yet, given that the fair-use standard is meant to serve as a "safety valve" between expression and copyright, problems regarding its effectiveness swiftly arise. Many contemporary secondary uses of copyrighted material (e.g., memes) are clearly within the ambit of critical expression, which, as shown above, is important because it is an essential component of the conditions conducive to individual and collective self-determination and equal participation in cultural meaning-making. However, often these contemporary secondary uses of copyrighted materials are typically not considered as such under fair use. In the spirit of safeguarding the higher-order conditions for free choice in the space of culture, then, secondary uses that are, say, comparatively less commercially successful or accepted than their mainstream copyrighted counterparts to which they allude should nonetheless be assessed equitably under the fair-use standard.

Mill's conception of speech goes hand-in-hand with democratizing copyright and aligning it with free-speech values vis-à-vis concepts of self-determination and cultural democracy. Specifically, ensuring that there be a robust "marketplace of ideas" in the broader search for truth necessarily includes prioritizing the critical conditions for genuine free choice (at both the individual and collective, cultural level). Moreover, the "marketplace of ideas" must be decentralized in terms of meaning-making and control

[70] *See* Balkin, *supra* note 23, at 35.

and equally accessible to all individuals. When the three chosen theories—Mill's "marketplace of ideas" rationale to free speech, self-determination theory of expression, and cultural democracy theory of expression—are welded together, the following framework for analysis emerges:

1. Individuals benefit from a diverse and robust "marketplace of ideas," which includes access to and free choice over ideas and options ranging from the eccentric and heterodox to the mainstream (i.e., subjectively preferred by the majority).
2. A wide range of possibilities, options, and alternatives is what makes individual choice and self-determination meaningful. That is, the individual is able to critically understand, evaluate, comment on the competing options and ideas as well as revise his or her conclusions and preferences about them. Extending that into the aggregate is what makes the search for "truth" via freedom of speech and expression possible.
3. Lastly, democratic culture, as a "realm of irreducible social interactions having powerful impact on individuals' sense of themselves,"[71] must be equally accessible to all individuals. That is, meaning-making through expression must be decentralized so that all individuals have the opportunity to shape, through expressive activity, others' subjective preferences that are formed from their own meaningful free choice.

In line with the above framework, the speech-and-copyright balance as manifested in today's application of fair use should be realigned with today's digital-era take on expressive activity, such that it continues to support notions of self-determination and cultural democracy. Given that modern technological infrastructure has greatly expanded the possibilities for individual participation in the growth and spread of culture and meaning-making, principles of copyright (e.g., where the conceptual line delineating "derivative" works from "fair uses" is drawn) should appropriately take into account these new critical methods of expressive

---

[71] Bracha & Syed, *supra* note 31, at 255.

activity that have, in a deeply democratic sense, emerged from mass participation in the cultural space of today's information society.

Therefore, the overarching priority for fair use, as a lever for balancing free expression and copyright interests, should be protecting the critical conditions that foster a democratic, decentralized culture of expression—i.e., a matrix of expression that is conducive to genuine, meaningful free choice and where meaning-making power is distributed equally among individuals.[72] Put simply, the fair-use standard must accurately appraise the value in collective meaning-making that collage and appropriation works potentially add to democratic culture.[73]

V. The Problem With The Modern-Day Application of Fair Use

a. A Survey of the Legal Landscape of Fair Use

While fair-use jurisprudence is generally headed in the direction of liberalizing and opening up of fair use,[74] there still remains a sizable degree of uncertainty with regard to whether internet-era appropriative/adaptive uses of copyrighted work qualify as "transformative" under fair use. To add to that, the Supreme Court has not yet weighed in on the question, so a great deal of discretion in interpreting the fair-use factors is left to the courts. The following is an analysis of a selection of cases—in chronological order—that hopefully highlights the issues that currently plague courts' application of fair use, including their test for assessing whether a given use is "transformative."[75] Much of the controlling case law is from the Second Circuit, whose jurisdiction is where much of the entertainment industry is situated.

---

[72] *See id.* at 263. ("[W]hen a specific feature of copyright has substantial effect on the higher-order conditions that validate individual preferences, there is nothing perverse in not subjecting this feature to the test of existing preferences.").

[73] *See id.*

[74] *See* Pam Samuelson, *Unbundling Fair Uses*, 77 FORDHAM L. REV. 2537 (2008) [hereinafter Samuelson].

[75] *See* Campbell v. Acuff-Rose Music, 510 U.S. 569, 579 (1994) (stating the test for transformative use).

The case *Rogers v. Koons*[76] illustrated that, at the time, a secondary work needed to be commenting on the original in order to be deemed transformative.[77] There, the Second Circuit held that Koons' sculpture did not qualify as a fair use.[78] Koons had removed the copyright label from a postcard and instructed his assistants to model the image into a sculpture.[78] He asked that as much detail be copied as possible while requesting some changes: that the puppies in the sculpture be made blue, their noses exaggerated, and flowers added to the hair of the man and women.[79] Rogers, the copyright owner of the photograph in the postcard, sued Koons. The Court here held that copying a photograph, when there is no clear need to imitate the photograph for parody, could lead to infringement liability.[80] It reasoned that Koons could have constructed his parody of that general type of art showcased in the postcard without copying the copyright holder's specific work.[81] Lastly, and perhaps most importantly, the court noted that Koons' work was not specifically commenting on the copyrighted work and therefore his use of the work could not be considered a transformative parodic fair use.[81]

In 2001, nine years after *Rogers*, the Eleventh Circuit stretched the meaning of "transformative" in its holding that the alleged infringement in question was a parodic fair use.[82] There, SunTrust Bank filed suit and a preliminary injunction against the defendant author's usage of a historical fiction book, *Gone With The Wind*, in her own book, *The Wind Done Gone*, over which Houghton Mifflin Co. had a copyright interest.[83] The infringing

---

[76] 960 F.2d 301 (2d Cir. 1992).

[77] *Id.* at 310.

[78] *Id.* at 306.

[78] *Id.* at 309.

[79] *Id.* at 305.

[80] *Id.* at 310.

[81] *Id.* ("[T]he copied work must be, at least in part, an object of the parody, otherwise there would be no need to conjure up the original work.").

[82] *See* SunTrust v. Houghton Mifflin Co., 268 F.3d 1257 (11th Cir. 2001).

[83] *Id.* at 1259.

work in question was a critique of *Gone With The Wind*'s depiction of slavery and the American South during the Civil-War era.[84] The defendant author of *The Wind Done Gone* used several characters, plot points, and major scenes from *Gone With The Wind* in the first half of her book.[85] The court determined that *The Wind Done Gone*, a parody of *Gone With The Wind*, would likely qualify as a fair use. It explained that for purposes of the fair-use analysis, a work is treated as a parody if "its aim is to *comment upon or criticize* a prior work by appropriating elements of the original in creating a new artistic, as opposed to scholarly or journalistic, work."[86] In other words, *The Wind Done Gone* would likely be considered a parodic fair use, not because it is a general commentary upon the Civil War-era American South, but rather because it is a criticism of and sharp riposte to the depiction of racial relations in *Gone With The Wind*.[87] The larger point arising from the court's reasoning here is that the creation and publication of a *carefully written* parody novel may count as fair use, that the commentary requirement for "transformative" parodic use may be fulfilled even if it involves directly copying from the original as a means to re-contextualize it.[88] Despite the author's heavy borrowing, the fact that the *The Wind Done Gone* tells a very different story in a very different voice as a means to criticize the original perhaps distinguishes it from the sculpture in *Rogers*.

In 2006, Koons' controversial artwork entered the judicial arena once again. Here, Koons had constructed a pictorial collage, using various photographs that included a copyrighted photograph owned by photographer Blanch.[89] Blanch's photograph portrayed a woman's legs reclining on a man's lap in an airplane cabin. Koons' collage included a cropped and re-oriented version of the photo, which was then placed among

---

84 *Id.* at 1270.

85 *Id.*

86 *Id.* at 1271 (emphasis added).

87 *Id.* at 1269.

88 *See id.* at 1270.

89 Blanch v. Koons, 396 F.Supp.2d 244, 247 (S.D.N.Y. 2005)

several other pairs of women's legs.[90] In an interesting change in direction, the Second Circuit affirmed the district court's summary-judgment holding that Koons' collage was a fair use.[91] The district court had distinguished this case from *Rogers* by asserting that Koons' collage uses the copyrighted photograph in order to create a new work of art with a distinct meaning, message, and character rather than merely offering a complete reproduction.[92] In the court's mind, Koons' collage did not appropriate any original, creative, or imaginative aspect of Blanch's photograph—that is, the collaged pairs of legs were shown to represent the social and aesthetic consequences of mass media, whereas the purpose of Blanch's photograph was to illustrate metallic nail polish.[93] The Second Circuit agreed, stating that Koons' collage used Blanch's work as "raw material, transform[ing] in the creation of new material, new aesthetics, new insights and understanding" rather than merely offering a complete reproduction."[94] In other words, the court found Koons' work to be transformative because it "add[ed] *value* to the original."[95]

However, what the court perceives as added, purpose-altering "value" is seemingly subjective. The reasoning employed by the court seems to be both heavy-handed and problematic. The court states, in pertinent part:

> [T]he use of a fashion photograph created for publication in a glossy American "lifestyles" magazine—with changes of its colors, the background against which it is portrayed, the medium, the size of the objects pictured, the objects' details and, crucially, their entirely different

---

[90] *Blanch*, 396 F.Supp.2d 476 at 249.

[91] *Id.* at 259.

[92] *Id.* at 481 (Koons' collage "does not 'supersede' or duplicate the objective of the original, but uses it as raw material in a novel context to create new information, new aesthetics, and new insights. Such use, whether successful or not artistically, is transformative.").

[93] *See id.* at 481.

[94] *Id.* at 251.

[95] *Id.* (emphasis added).

> purpose and meaning—as part of a massive painting commissioned for exhibition in a German art-gallery space. We therefore conclude that the use in question was transformative.[96]

Who is to say, for example, that Koons' alteration of the image in the image in *Rogers* does not constitute use of "'raw material' in the furtherance of distinct creative and communicative objectives" so as to render it transformative? The court's reliance on the parody–satire distinction in *Rogers* would certainly not take kindly to modern-day expressive activity. Koons' use of the copyrighted image in modeling his infringing sculpture is strikingly similar to how memes are made online—how bits of media are cobbled together, superimposed, and repackaged such that the context is markedly altered, yet the emerging commentary is perhaps not so clear (at least not as clear as Koons' collage). Since many memes today—perhaps through the addition of a vague, apolitical caption or the superimposition of a psychedelic filter onto copyrighted work(s)—add meaning in a way that is difficult to reduce into exact, *Blanch*-like[97] themes, it is quite possible that they would meet the same fate as that of the sculpture in *Rogers*. Therefore, applying the *Blanch* conception of fair use to appropriation and collage works online could chill people's ability to engage in meaningful expression and participate in the formation of culture—the critical conditions of copyright and free speech that fair use is charged to protect.

In 2010, the Second Circuit ruled on a case that was factually similar to *SunTrust*; however, it found an opposite ruling.[99] Here, the defendant author Colting wrote and published a book called *60 Years Later: Coming through the Rye*. Colting's book was framed as a sequel to *Catcher in the Rye*, taking up the story of Holden Caulfield as the 76-year-old "Mr. C."[98] The author of *Catcher in the Rye*, J.D. Salinger, too, is featured as 90-

---

[96] *Id.* at 253.

[97] That is, the Second Circuit is easily able to articulate the difference in purpose of use between the copyrighted and secondary works: the pair of legs in Blanch's photograph is used to showcase metallic nail polish, whereas in Koons' collage, they are used alongside other pairs of legs as a means to criticize the nature of mass media.

[98] *See* Salinger v. Colting, 607 F.3d 68, 71 (2d Cir. 2012).

year-old, "fictionalized" author in the book, who "has been haunted by his creation and now wishes to bring him back to life in order to kill him."[99] Throughout Colting's work, Mr. C recounts the events that occurred in *Catcher in the Rye*, exhibiting the famous characters' eccentricities that were noted in the original work. Colting's work also uses many of the same plot points and scenes.[100] However, Colting responded by denying that his work was meant to be a sequel, rather it was a "'critical examination of the character Holden and the way he is portrayed in [*Catcher in the Rye*], the relationship between Salinger and his iconic creation, and the life of a particular author as he grows old but remains imprisoned by the literary character he created.'"[101] He also noted that, among other things, Mr. C undergoes significant character development, ending up with a life that is complete apart from *Catcher in the Rye*.[102] In fact, one of the two literary experts testifying on Colting's behalf described his work as a "meta-commentary."[103]

Despite this, the Second Circuit affirmed the lower court's preliminary injunction. Importantly, in applying *Campbell*, the lower court held that purpose and character of the use in Colting's work was "not sufficiently 'transformative.'"[104] Moreover, it similarly concluded that the work did "not have sufficiently non-parodic transformative value," though without much explanation.[105] Interestingly, as was the case in *SunTrust*, Colting heavily borrowed from *Catcher in the Rye* in terms of substance and style and told a very different story in a very different voice. However, unlike the defendant author in *SunTrust*, Colting could not rely on fair use for protection. As far as the Second Circuit was concerned, Colting's *SunTrust*-like re-contextualization and reframing of an earlier author's work

---

[99] *Id.* at 71–72.

[100] *Id.* at 72.

[101] *Id.* (internal citations omitted).

[102] *Id.*

[103] *Id.* (internal quotations omitted).

[104] *Id.* at 73.

[105] *Id.*

was not enough. Therefore, the difference in the Eleventh's and Second Circuit's interpretation of factually similar cases is noteworthy.

In 2013, the Second Circuit took a groundbreaking approach to fair use when it held in *Cariou v. Prince*[106] that a secondary use need not comment on or critique the original to be transformative, so long as it produces a new message.[107] Here, plaintiff and professional photographer Cariou published a book of portraits and landscape photographs titled "Yes, Rasta."[108] Prince, a well-known appropriation artist, altered a number of Cariou's photographs and incorporated them into a series of paintings and collages, titled "Canal Zone."[109] Soon after, Cariou sued Prince, among others, for copyright infringement. In response to Cariou's claim, the defendants raised the defense of fair use.[110]

The Second Circuit overruled the lower court's holding and held in favor of the defendants, concluding that "Canal Zone" constituted fair use for several reasons. First, the court emphasized that "the law imposes no requirement that a work comment on the original or its author in order to be considered transformative, and [that] a secondary work may constitute a fair use even if it serves some purpose other than those (criticism, comment, news reporting, teaching, scholarship, and research) identified in the preamble to the statute."[111] Interestingly, this line of reasoning is opposite from the reasoning relied upon in *Salinger* and *Rogers*. Quoting *Campbell*, the court held that, as long as a new work generally alters the original with "new expression, meaning, or message," it qualifies as a fair use.[112] In doing so, the Second Circuit greatly expanded the *Campbell* standard of what adding "new expression, meaning, or message" could

[106] 714 F.3d 694, 706 (2d Cir. 2013).

[107] *Id.* at 706.

[108] *Cariou*, 714 F.3d at 698.

[109] *Id.*

[110] *Id.* at 698–99.

[111] *Id.*

[112] *Id.* at 706.

mean—that is, a use devoid of commentary could now qualify. (Recall in *Salinger*, the district court—whose ruling was affirmed by the Second Circuit—relied on *Campbell* and uses that very same phrase to justify a denial of fair use for a work that offered commentary to a similar degree to *The Wind Done Gone* in *SunTrust*.)[113]

Second, the court determined that the majority of Prince's works demonstrated a drastically different approach and aesthetic from Cariou's, implying that the *visual* juxtaposition between the two artists' works (sans any comment or critique of *Yes, Rasta* on Canal Zone's part) was enough to be deemed transformative. To illustrate, the court stated: "Where Cariou's serene and deliberately composed portraits and landscape photographs depict the natural beauty of Rastafarians and their surrounding environs, Prince's crude and jarring works, on the other hand, are hectic and provocative."[114] The court delved deeper into the specifics by taking note of the fact that Cariou's black-and-white photographs were printed in a 9.5"x12" book, whereas Prince's collages were placed on canvas that "incorporate color, feature distorted human and other forms and settings, and measure between ten and nearly a hundred times the size of the photographs."[115] Prince's composition, presentation, scale, color palette, and media were, in the court's view, fundamentally different and new compared to Cariou's work, as was the *expressive* nature of Prince's works.[116] Crucially, the court's interpretation opened up the possibility for conflating "transformative" use with a visual alteration of an original work. It also allowed for the expansion of the definition of "transformative" to include uses that are solely visual (i.e., without commentary) in nature.

Third, the Second Circuit held that artworks should be examined as they would "reasonably be perceived" in order to assess their transformative nature.[117] In the court's words: "What is critical is how the work in question appears to the reasonable observer, not simply what an

---

[113] *Id.*

[114] *Id.*

[115] *Id.*

[116] *Id.*

[117] *Id.* at 707.

artist might say about a particular piece or body of work."[118] That is, the focus of the fair-use inquiry should shift away from the singular, subjective intent of the putative fair user and towards a more *audience-focused* inquiry. Even though Prince expressly stated that he did not "have a message," the court still concluded that reasonably situated observers would see "Canal Zone" as having a radically different purpose and aesthetic than Cariou's *Yes, Rasta*.[120] This alone was enough to render Prince's works "transformative."

The expansive conception of fair use under *Cariou*, however, was rather short lived. In late 2016, the Second Circuit pared down the fair-use standard in *TCA Television Corp. v. McCollum*.[119] Here, the defendant producers of the Broadway show, "Hand of God" were sued for copyright infringement for their use of the famous Abbott & Costello "Who's on First?" comedy routine in a portion of their Play.[120] Despite its prior holding in *Cariou*, the court reversed the trial court's findings that the defendants' use of the comedy routine qualified as a non-infringing fair use.[121] In doing so, the court clarified the limits of transformative use, cutting back on what had been viewed by many as an increasingly expansive application of the term in fair use cases.

The district court had found that the use of the skit in the Play was so "highly transformative" as to support a fair-use defense because by having a simple character perform the comedy skit, the Play's authors were able to juxtapose, through use of the sock puppet, "Jason's seemingly soft-spoken personality [with] the actual outrageousness of his inner nature."[122] Moreover, the district court explained that this contrast was "a darkly comedic critique of the social norms governing a small town in the Bible Belt."[123] The Second Circuit criticized the district court's reasoning as

---

118 *Id.*

119 TCA Television Corp. v. McCollum, 839 F.3d 168 (2d Cir. 2016).

120 *Id.* at 172.

121 *Id.*

122 TCA Television Corp. v. McCollum, 151 F.Supp.3d 419, 434–35 (S.D.N.Y. 2015).

123 *Id.* at 434–35.

being "flawed in that what it identifies are the general artistic and critical purpose and character of the Play. The district court did not explain how defendants' extensive copying of a famous comedy routine was necessary to this purpose, much less how the character of [Abbott & Costello's comedy skit] was transformed by the defendants' use."[124] It is unclear, however, whether a court in its fair-use inquiry is required to articulate a reason why a given secondary use is "necessary" to the purpose of the work. Surely Prince's use of Cariou's photographs was not "necessary" in the way the Second Circuit here means it. On the contrary, Prince's appropriation of Cariou's photographs was arguably more arbitrary than the secondary use at issue here. Even so, as for surmising why a secondary use may be "necessary" to the purpose of the secondary work, the district court did in fact state that "*Hand to God* uses the [comedy routine] to create context and 'a background for the ever more sinister character development of Tyrone, the alter-ego sock puppet.'"[125]

Not surprisingly, the district court's overall conclusion that the defendants' use of the comedy skit was "transformative" was based on its interpretation of *Cariou*, which cast away reliance on the rigid satire–parody distinction. The court operated on the assumption that commentary is not necessary for the fair-use defense and that whether a use of the original is "transformative" should be based on a "reasonable perception" of the new work.[126] Accordingly, the court concluded the following regarding the use of the comedy routine: "It is the performance through the anti-hero puppet, Tyrone, that according to the Defendants, creates new aesthetics and understandings about the relationships between horror and comedy that are absent from Abbott and Costello's performances of the Routine in *One Night* and *The Naughty Nineties*."[127] In its view, the court determined that the tone of the actor reenacting the comedy skit was markedly different. Furthermore, it identified the purpose underlying the "Hand of God" producers' use of the comedy skit in question, stating, "While the [comedy routine], as performed in the play, also results in comic

---

[124] *TCA Television Corp.*, 839 F.3d 168 at 179.

[125] *TCA Television Corp.*, 151 F.Supp.3d at 436.

[126] *Id.* at 435.

[127] *Id.* at 436.

relief for the audience, it does so for reasons different from why audiences found the original sketch humorous."[128] From there, the court went into granular detail as to how the new work's use of the comedy routine, from the perspective of a reasonable observer, was humorous in a fundamentally different way than in the original.[129]

Using *Campbell* for support, the Second Circuit emphasized that under the first fair-use factor, the purpose and character of the use, the focus of inquiry "is not simply on the new work, i.e., on whether that work serves a purpose or conveys an overall expression, meaning, or message different from the copyrighted material it appropriates. Rather, the critical inquiry is whether the new work uses the copyrighted material itself for a purpose, or imbues it with a character, different from that for which it was created."[130] So, even if the district court found that *Hand to God* is a "darkly comedic critique of the social norms governing a small town in the Bible Belt," and "the Play's purpose and character are completely different from the vaudevillian humor originally animating Who's on First?, that, by itself, does not demonstrate that defendants' use of the [comedy routine] in the Play was transformative of the original work."[131] Basically, the district court's reasoning that the purpose of the secondary use was to incite a certain kind of humor, thereby significantly different from the purpose for which the original was created, did not convince the Second Circuit.[132]

Lastly, the Second Circuit went to great lengths to distinguish this case from *Cariou*. It asserted that the challenged artworks in *Cariou*

---

[128] *Id.* at 437.

[129] *See id.* ("Tyrone, the sock puppet, breaks the 'fourth wall' with the audience when he says to Jessica, 'You'd know [Jason didn't make the Routine up] if you weren't so stupid,' sharing with them an inside joke. The audience laughs at Jason's lie, not, as Plaintiffs claim, simply the words of the Routine itself. For the lie to be apparent, the play requires that the audience be able to recognize the original source of Jason's sock puppet performance. This statutory factor, therefore, weighs strongly in favor of Defendants.") (internal citations omitted).

[130] *TCA Television Corp.*, 839 F.3d 168 at 180.

[131] *Id.*

[132] Madison, *Rewriting Fair Use* at 407.

satisfied the *Campbell* standard because "they not only strove for 'new aesthetics with creative and communicative results distinct from' that of the copyrighted material, but also gave the incorporated photographs 'new expression,' thereby admitting a transformative purpose."[133] Unlike the producers' use of the Abbott & Costello routine, Prince's use of Cariou's photographs so "'heavily obscured and altered' the original photographs as to make them 'barely recognizable' within the new work" and therefore "transformative" in its purpose of use.[134] The court heavily relied on the phrase "barely recognizable," which appears only once in *Cariou.*[135]

While the take on fair use in *Cariou* is comparatively broad, it does suffer from relying on the same distinction that was made in *Blanch* between "raw" and "cooked" culture. To provide context, in describing the drastic change in aesthetics depicted in Prince's "Canal Zone," the Second Circuit points out that while "*the entire source photograph is used*[] it is also heavily obscured and altered to the point that Cariou's original is barely recognizable."[136] Even though the Second Circuit in *TCA Television Corp.* zeroed in on certain phrasing made in *Cariou*, it still did not address, as the lower court did, the broader implications of *Cariou*'s holdings—e.g., that whether a purpose of use is "transformative" should be based on a "reasonable perception" of the new work. Therefore, even though this court armed itself with a narrower construction of the *Campbell* standard (i.e., that the "critical inquiry is whether the new work uses the copyrighted material itself for a purpose, or imbues it with a character, different from that for which it was created"), one might point out that it did not evaluate, through the lens of a "reasonable" observer, whether the use of the comedy routine was done for a different purpose than the original. It should also be noted that the district court identified a possible purpose for using the skit

---

[133] *TCA Television Corp.*, 839 F.3d 168 at 180.

[134] *Id.*

[135] *Id.* at 18 ("The Play may convey a dark critique of society, but it does not transform Abbott and Costello's Routine so that it conveys that message. To the contrary, it appears that the Play specifically has its characters perform *Who's on First?* without alteration so that the audience will readily recognize both the famous [comedy skit] and the boy's false claim to having created it.").

[136] *Cariou*, 714 F.3d, at 710.

that was different than the reason the skit was originally created.[137] Lastly, this case stands at odds with the Eleventh Circuit's *SunTrust* (where the *The Wind Done Gone*, which heavily borrowed from *Gone With The Wind*, was deemed a parodic fair use).

Perhaps the Second Circuit's approach in this case can be explained by the fact that *Cariou* drew a great deal of criticism from practitioners. Many pointed out that the definition of "transformative" use was expanding into areas of artistic appropriation that previously would have been well over the line into infringement. Several notable commentators looked at that case as a substantial expansion, and some suggested that a re-examination might be appropriate.[138] *TCA Television Corp.* can certainly be read as the court's response to that criticism: A pulling back from the expansion of "transformative" fair use.

b. Identified Inconsistencies & Issues

From the selection of cases above, several issues arise in how fair use is applied in practice as a mechanism to balance free expression and copyright. First, there is a significant degree of uncertainty and variance among courts' approach to applying fair use and determining whether a certain use is "transformative." Indeed, as Madison puts it:

> The "transformative use" standard that the Court in *Campbell* borrowed from Judge Leval has been interpreted widely, and wrongly, as validating precisely this approach to fair use. If the defendant's work "transforms" the plaintiff's work, then the defendant wins. It is possible to use this test to reach sensible results, but the reasoning in these cases seems tortured, and it's difficult to implement the rule on a universal basis. How transformative is transformative enough? No one ever knows until the appellate court sings.[139]

---

[137] *See* Madison, *supra* note 17.

[138] *TCA Television Corp.*, 839 F.3d at 181.

[139] *See* Madison, *supra* note 17.

Although scholars such as Pam Samuelson argue that fair-use law is both more coherent and more predictable than many commentators have previously perceived—that fair-uses cases indeed tend to fall into common patterns and policy-relevant clusters—this is certainly not the case with transformative appropriations such as the those in *Rogers* and *Blanch,* or non-parodic transformation critiques of an earlier author's work such as the those in *SunTrust* and *Campbell.*[140] In fact, Samuelson specifically acknowledges that there is much more fair-use-related risk when it comes to transformative adaptations.[141] Therefore, despite the gradual liberalization of fair use, significant uncertainty remains with respect to certain critical secondary uses of existing works.

Connecting the discussion back to expressive activity pursued by today's information society via contemporary collage and appropriation art forms, it is important to note that the uncertainty hovering over whether a work is "transformative" enough will tend to hurt the flourishing of these art forms. To illustrate, remixes and mashups—expressive works that re-contextualize parts of existing works—might very well be perceived by the public to shed new light on and contribute new insights about the original. However, under *TCA Television Corp.*, a given remix may not be perceived by a court to meet the "barely recognizable" benchmark in relation to the original work. Equally possible, the purpose underlying the remix's use of the original work may not be obvious enough for a court to conclude that it is sufficiently "different from that for which it was created"—*even if* reasonable individuals interacting and communicating with each other on the digital speech-culture matrix would collectively agree that the remix is a "transformative" use of the original.

Second, the uncertainty described above not only leads to the chilling of certain expressive activities, but it also undermines the commitment to safeguard critical conditions of individual and collective free choice as well as the decentralization of meaning-making—i.e., the shared goal of free speech and copyright under consequence-sensitive democratic theories of expression. Relatedly, uncertainty in the reliability of fair use as a standard will diminish the robustness of the "marketplace of ideas" and endanger people's capacity to make meaningful choices with respect to expression. Legal scholars Robert H. Mnookin and Lewis

---

[140] *See* Samuelson, *supra* note 74, at 2553.

[141] Samuelson, *supra* note 74, at 2553.

Kornhauser contend that such a "'shadow' of the law [can] exert[] an indirect influence on bargaining and decision making."[142] Indeed, there are plenty of examples in the music industry that speak to the chilling effect of the "shadow" cast by a broken fair use.[143] The overuse of cease and desists in the creative industry provides even more fodder for this notion.[144] Popular mashup artists such as Girl Talk and Illegal Art, for example, have stated that if they were ever to be sued for copyright infringement, they would hope for a cease and desist letter first.[145] Of course, many artists choose to bypass the risk altogether and simply resist making the kind of art that may violate copyright. Indeed, one can see for themselves the deterring effect of the culture of C&Ds by visiting the Chilling Effect

---

142 Dembers, *supra* note 37, at 10.

143 Some notable examples include: (1) In the middle of 2001, Mariah Carey released her first single from *Glitter*, entitled "Loverboy," which featured a sample of "Firecracker" by Yellow Magic Orchestra. A month later, Jennifer Lopez released "I'm Real" with the same "Firecracker" sample. Carey quickly discarded it and replaced it with "Candy" by Cameo. (2) In 2001, Armen Boladian and his company Bridgeport Music Inc. filed over 500 copyright infringement suits against 800 artists using samples from George Clinton's catalogue. (3) Public Enemy recorded a track entitled "Psycho of Greed" (2002) for their album *Revolverlution* that contained a continuous looping sample from The Beatles' track "Tomorrow Never Knows." However, the clearance fee demanded by Capitol Records and the surviving Beatles was so high that the group decided to pull the track from the album. (4) Danger Mouse with the release of *The Grey Album* in 2004, which is a remix of The Beatles' self-titled album and rapper Jay-Z's *The Black Album* has been embroiled in a similar situation with the record label EMI issuing cease and desist orders over uncleared Beatles samples. (5) On March 19, 2006, a judge ordered that sales of The Notorious B.I.G.'s album *Ready to Die* be halted because the title track sampled a 1972 song by the Ohio Players, "Singing in the Morning," without permission. (6) On November 20, 2008, electronic band Kraftwerk convinced the German Federal Supreme Court that even the smallest shreds of sounds ("Tonfetzen") are "copyrightable" (e.g. protected), and that sampling a few bars of a drum beat can be an infringement. (7) In 2011, Lynn Tolliver won a $1.2 million lawsuit over unauthorized sampling of his song "I Need a Freak," most notably used by Black Eyed Peas in the song "My Humps." The song was back in court in 2014 over royalty issues.

144 *See* Regina Schaffer–Goldman, *Cease-and-Desist: Tarnishment's Blunt Sword in Its Battle Against the Unseemly, the Unwholesome, and the Unsavory*, 20 FORDHAM INTEL. PROP. ENT. L. J. 1243 (2010).

145 Ryan Dombal, Interviews: Girl Talk, PITCHFORK (Aug. 30, 2006), http://pitchfork.com/features/interviews/6415-girl-talk/; *see also,* Kerri Eble, *This Is A Remix: Remixing Music Copyright To Better Protect Mashup Artists*, U. of IL. L. REV. 661 (2013).

Clearinghouse website, which catalogues and displays thousands of letters that are sent to companies and individuals.[146] Lastly—though beyond the scope of this essay—it helps to note that, under the Digital Millennium Copyright Act, the fair-use defense must be considered by the copyright holder before requesting a takedown,[147] yet fear of litigation still drives online platforms like SoundCloud and YouTube to over-censor contested content via their DMCA takedown procedures in lieu of investigating the merits of the request.[148]

Third, the uncertainty inherent in courts' application of fair use is further exacerbated by the procedural treatment of fair use in the judicial system. Under the fair-use doctrine, a defendant bears the burden of proving that her use of copyrighted material merits protection as speech. Unlike other speech contexts, the burden of proving the protected nature of expression lies with the speaker.[149] This burden of proof chills fair-use

---

[146] The Chilling Effects Clearinghouse is "[a] joint project of the Electronic Frontier Foundation and Harvard, Stanford, Berkeley, University of San Francisco, University of Maine, George Washington School of Law, and Santa Clara University School of Law clinics." CHILLING EFFECTS CLEARINGHOUSE, http://www.chillingeffects.org (last visited Apr. 7, 2010).

[147] Lenz v. Universal Music Corp., 815 F.3d 1145, 1152–53 (9th Cir. 2015).

[148] *See* Tim Cushing, *Soundcloud Has Given Universal Music Group The Ability To Directly Remove Content*, TECHDIRT (July 2, 2014), https://www.techdirt.com/articles/20140702/10252827760/soundcloud-has-given-universal-music-group-ability-to-directly-remove-content.shtml ("Now, there's more bad news for users of SoundCloud's service. Apparently, Universal Music Group has the power to directly pull tracks without issuing a takedown request to SoundCloud. This has resulted in a paying customer of SoundCloud having his account deleted for copyright violations with the only recourse available being to contact Universal directly to dispute the takedown."); *see also* Jeffrey Yau, *Soundcloud Starting To Ban Users For Reposting Too Much*, YOUR EDM (Oct. 31, 2015) ("Users who have reposted heavily in short periods of time are starting to receive messages from SoundCloud stating that their account "loses that human feeling" which has resulted in a number of temporary bans."); Harley Brown, *Ten DJs and Producers Discuss SoundCloud's Future*, SPIN (Aug. 26, 2015), https://www.spin.com/2015/08/djs-soundcloud-q-a-read-zeds-dead/; Alfred C. Yen, *Eldred, the First Amendment, and Aggressive Copyright Claims*, 40 HOUS. L. REV. 673, 673–74 (2003).

[149] *Proving Fair Use*, *supra* note 36, at 1782.

expression.[150] It likely causes self-censorship because "it plays such a significant role in the judicial analysis of whether a use is fair."[151] Indeed, the fair-use analysis centers around issues of fact, and those issues naturally breed uncertainty because of their subjective and speculative natures. Nonetheless, it is the fair user who bears the burden of establishing factual answers.[152] To succeed in this endeavor, the fair user has to "produce the necessary evidence (even where the inquiry is speculative) and persuade the court that her interpretation of the evidence reflects fact (even where the inquiry is subjective).[153] In effect, the burden of proof assignment in the context of fair use assigns a loser by default, and as it turns out, overcoming this default presumption is a near impossibility for fair users because the very definition of fairness is vague. As such, the fair user is more likely than not to be penalized when fact-finders face uncertainty over issues in the fair-use analysis, despite the fact that fair use itself is an inherently vague doctrine.

This placement of burden of proof, in combination with advances in technology, adds fuel to the fire. As legal scholar Ned Snow writes:

> With the rise of the Internet, individual fair users can now reach large audiences at no cost . . . As a result, copyright holders now receive notice of individuals' unauthorized uses; copyright holders can and do track individuals' copying activities, and they threaten suits against individuals . . . A copyright holder has every incentive to silence a scathing criticism of her work, even if that criticism is a fair use, and Internet technology makes pursuit of that silence possible. A copyright holder who pursues an individual fair user will nearly always be

---

[150] *See Proving Fair Use*, *supra* note 36, at 1795 ("Supreme Court jurisprudence in the *New York Times v. Sullivan* line of case law supports the view that a burden of proof may unconstitutionally chill protected speech.").

[151] *Proving Fair Use*, *supra* note 36, at 1783.

[152] *See Proving Fair Use*, *supra* note 36, at 1783; *see also* Joseph P. Liu, Copyright and Breathing Space, 30 COLUM. J.L. & ARTS 429, 443–44 (2007) (explaining that the fourth fair-use factor often turns on speculative claims of market harm).

[153] *Proving Fair Use*, *supra* note 36, at 1783

> successful at achieving the desired silence. The burden of proof imposes a high financial cost on the fair user to gather evidence and persuade a fact-finder of its correct interpretation. This cost becomes prohibitive as individual fair users often lack economic means to defend their speech."[154]

Usage of online tracking technologies has made individual fair users increasingly subject to the scrutiny of overzealous copyright holders, so much so that the decision to self-censor often becomes automatic under such a "shadow of the law." The heightened chance of facing claims of copyright infringement, along with the heavy burden of proof imposed on fair users, considerably deters many would-be fair users from participating in certain critical expressive activities.[155] What this does, of course, is impermissibly frustrate the shared goal of the First Amendment and copyright and cut against democratic theories of expression's deep concern for safeguarding critical conditions of meaningful self-determination and equal participation in culture.

VI. Recommendation: A Two-Part Proposal For Fair Use Reform

In light of the foregoing, this essay recommends the following two-part proposal for reforming fair use's treatment of contemporary collage and appropriation works of expression:

1. Embrace an interpretation of "transformative" fair use that is close to that of *Cariou*. For a secondary use to be deemed "transformative," it need not comment on or critique the original, so long as it adds something new, with a further purpose or different character, altering the first with new expression, meaning or message.[156] Such uses can include

---

[154] *Proving Fair Use*, *supra* note 36, at 1805–06.

[155] Eugene Volokh, *Freedom of Speech and Intellectual Property: Some Thoughts After Eldred, 44 Liquormart, and Bartnicki*, 40 Hous. L. Rev. 697, 721 (2003).

[156] *See* Cariou v. Prince, 714 F.3d 694, 705–06 ("The law imposes no requirement that a work comment on the original or its author in order to be considered transformative, and a secondary work may constitute a fair use even if it serves some purpose other than those

incorporating an original work into different artistic context such that it materially changes how the work's aesthetics are perceived. Furthermore (and more importantly), fair use should be an audience-focused inquiry. Whether the secondary use in question is "transformative" should depend on how it may "reasonably be perceived," not on the appropriative artist's subjective intentions.[157] As long as the borrower has a reasonably perceivable "general creative rationale"[158] for using an original work and the use in some way new meaning—perhaps through message or context—to the original, the use should be deemed transformative.

2. Shift the procedural burden of proof from the fair user onto the copyright holder. Where there is uncertainty in a question of fact over whether a use is fair—e.g., whether a use is sufficiently "transformative"—a finding of fair use should be favored over that of infringement. Accordingly, the copyright holder will be charged with resolving any factual uncertainties in order to successfully fulfill his or her burden of showing infringement.

The main vision of this doctrinal and procedural proposal is that it will enable fair use—a vastly important feature of copyright—to

---

(criticism, comment, news reporting, teaching, scholarship, and research) identified in the preamble to the statute. Instead, as the Supreme Court as well as decisions from our court have emphasized, to qualify as a fair use, a new work generally must alter the original with 'new expression, meaning, or message.'") (internal citations omitted).

[157] *Id.* at 707 ("Rather than confining our inquiry to Prince's explanations of his artworks, we instead examine how the artworks may 'reasonably be perceived' in order to assess their transformative nature.").

[158] *See* Blanch v. Koons, 467 F.3d 244, 255 ("It is not, of course, our job to judge the merits of 'Niagara,' or of Koons's approach to art."); Campbell v. Acuff-Rose Music, 510 U.S. 569, 582 ("[I]t would be a dangerous undertaking for persons trained only to the law to constitute themselves final judges of the worth of a work, outside of the narrowest and most obvious limits.") (quoting Bleistein v. Donaldson Lithographing Co., 188 U.S. 239, 251 (1903) (Holmes, J.))). The question is whether Koons had a genuine creative rationale for borrowing Blanch's Image, rather than using it merely "to get attention or to avoid the drudgery in working up something fresh." *Id.* at 580. "Although it seems clear enough to us that Koons' use of a slick fashion photograph enables him to satirize life as it appears when seen through the prism of slick fashion photography, we need not depend on our own poorly honed artistic sensibilities."

appropriately and equitably balance free speech with copyright values in today's information era and further the goal of safeguarding the free and widespread dissemination of expression and ideas.

VII. JUSTIFICATION FOR THE TWO-PART PROPOSAL

a. Part I of the Proposal (doctrinal)

The proposed doctrinal change to courts' interpretations of what constitutes a sufficiently "transformative" purpose for a given secondary use is supported by the chosen theories of analysis. The proliferation of digital technologies has unlocked new spaces in critical expression, particularly with respect to contemporary collage and appropriation art forms. Accordingly, such forms of critical and collective expression should be recognized by the fair-use standard. An expansive, *Cariou*-like conception of "transformative" fair use—venturing beyond the limitations of the parody–satire distinction and courts' apparent need for the difference in purpose between the secondary work's use and the original to be blatantly obvious—would allow for fair use's speech-and-copyright balancing function to realign with today's technological realities. Indeed, there are many forms of collage and appropriation art whose alterations (including the reasons behind the alterations) cannot be adequately described in thematic, archetypal terms. An expansive standard of fair use would, in effect, ensure that these new forms of art are not silenced from the outset. In doing so, it would support the critical conditions necessary for self-determination and equal participation in culture as well as further the shared goal of the First Amendment and copyright (i.e., safeguarding the free and widespread dissemination of expression and ideas).

As the Second Circuit acknowledged in *Blanch*, "[T]ransformative works . . . lie at the heart of the fair use doctrine's guarantee of breathing space . . . ."[159] Expanding "transformative" fair use to include contemporary appropriation art that challenge the way people think about not just art, but also objects, images, sound, and culture, will preserve an individual's right to self-determination and ability to construct meaning by way of

[159] Blanch v. Koons, 467 F.3d 244, 251 (2d Cir. 2006).

participating in the ever-evolving matrix of culture. Allowing the fair-use standard to grow stale, and as a result, chill of various forms of expression will produce a dull world where individual choice is not meaningful or autonomous. First, the range of competing options and ideas available for choosing will be severely limited as a result of fair use skewing copyright interests against new forms of expressive activity. Second, unaware of all of the possible alternatives, individuals will neither be able to critically reflect upon and understand the options given to them, nor will they be able to form preferences and influence others meaningfully through cultural interaction. Third, in the midst of a dwindling "marketplace of ideas"—where expressive works depicting dissenting ideas, which could be of potential value to cultural discourse, are increasingly silenced—the "Millian" search for truth will come to a screeching halt. Fourth, objectively beneficial heterodox forms of online-era expression will fail to meet an increasingly outdated fair-use standard and possibly taper off into extinction. Therefore, ensuring that fair use is designed to create "ample space for critical expression is crucial to nourishing the conditions of genuine free choice and meaningful decision-making with respect to expression."[160]

Assessing whether a use is "transformative" through the lens of a reasonable observer is in line with the chosen democratic theories of expression: the cultural democracy and self-determination theories of copyright as well as Mill's conception of free speech. If fair use is indeed a mechanism that serves to balance (1) the public interest in free expression—i.e., the means by which people navigate and interact within the omnipotent cultural swirl of icons, symbols, brands, ideas, etc.—with (2) incentivizing the creation of work by protecting private interest in copyright, it makes sense that whether a given expressive activity is "fair" should be assessed in the aggregate, against an objective standard. An audience-focused inquiry of fair use would therefore constitute a stronger, more predictable standard for application. This is because the "reasonable person" standard is thought to capture cultural norms. Now, the fair-use inquiry would take into account the democratic culture's wider perception of whether an added new meaning qualifies as "transformative." In effect, an audience-focused fair-use standard would make it far more likely that

[160] Bracha & Syed, *supra* note 31, at 262.

critical, legitimate secondary uses of existing works are exempted from copyright liability.

The speech-culture matrix in which all individuals operate and interact—what all individuals experience as social reality—is a "constellation of cultural structures that we ourselves construct and transform in ongoing practice."[161] As social agents, individuals are constantly engaged in a continuous process—both online and offline—of constructing and comprehending the meaning of symbols. In doing so, individuals collectively "give meaning to the objective world and define their own identity."[162] Therefore, interpreting fair use through broader cultural norms would dramatically lower the risk of litigation and encourage individuals to participate in cultural meaning-making through critical expressive activity. Put differently, analyzing whether a secondary use can "reasonably be perceived" to have, say, altered an existing work with a new meaning would enhance the predictability in outcome for fair use. Ultimately, an expanded, more democratic version of the fair-use standard would bring it much be closer towards striking a perfect balance between the speech-suppressive position of copyright and the speech-protective position of free speech.

b. Part II of the Proposal (procedural)

In combination with the proposed doctrinal changes to fair use, courts should shift the placement of the burden of proof from the fair user to the copyright holder asserting infringement. Given that the fair-use inquiry is fundamentally characterized by factual uncertainty, it should be procedurally structured in a way that it *reduces*, rather than magnifies, the likelihood of self-censorship among would-be fair users. As has been reiterated throughout this essay, the chilling of critical expressive activity—here, stemming from the procedural design of today's fair-use standard—impermissibly undercuts the shared goal of free speech and copyright.

---

[161] Rosemary J. Coombe, *Objects of Property and Subjects of Politics: Intellectual Property Laws and Democratic Dialogue*, 69 TEXAS L. REV. 1853, 1858 (1991).

[162] Elkin-Koren, *Cyberlaw and Social Change*, *supra* note 58, at 233.

Policy-wise, flipping the placement of the burden of proof in fair use would be a welcome step towards protecting fair users, rather than punishing them. A proliferation of secondary uses as a result of the shift would certainly increase the range of possibilities in the "marketplace of ideas," making it more likely that more heterodox expressions will be able to enter the fray and make individual choice more meaningful. In the words of Mill: "Precisely because the tyranny of opinion is such as to make eccentricity a reproach, it is desirable, in order to break through the tyranny, that people should be eccentric."[163]

So far, it has been established that, in ideal conditions, the Free Speech Clause and the Copyright Clause further the same goal of encouraging meaningful creation of, and equal access to, works of expression, a goal that was assigned to them by the Framers at the time of their constitutional conception. The chosen critical theories of analysis lend further credence to that idea. Fair use, acting as a "safety valve" as means to protect the ideal conditions in which free speech and copyright are harmonized, lies at the heart of the matter. Its burden of proof does as well.[164] Therefore, it makes sense that, if the burden of proof in other speech contexts (e.g., defamation) that deal with reconciling private versus public interests is placed on the private actor, then the burden of proof in the context of fair use (also having to reconcile private versus public interests) is placed on the copyright holder alleging infringement.

The Supreme Court's jurisprudence in the *New York Times v. Sullivan*[165] line of cases presents the view that "a burden of proof may unconstitutionally chill protected speech . . . the law should not require a speaker to bear the burden of proving the legitimacy of her speech."[166] This is certainly the principle that courts follow in the defamation context, and

---

[163] *See* Cate, *supra* note 46, at 62.

[164] *Proving Fair Use*, *supra* note 36, at 1791.

[165] 376 U.S. 254 (1964).

[166] *Id.* at 1795.

there is a strong argument for applying it in the context of fair use.[167] Consider the broad, thematic commonalities between libel and fair use: much like with libel, the fact-finding process in fair use is frequently, if not constantly, mired by factual uncertainties. The burden placement in the libel context sends a message suggesting that the interest in the public access to speech (especially speech that constitutes matters of public concern) presumptively outweighs the private interest in suppressing speech through a libel claim. Likewise, when it comes to protecting speech against suppression, the burden of proof should rest with the copyright holder showing that the interest in protecting expression outweighs the private interest in getting compensated for copyright infringement.[168] In both contexts, the placing the burden of proof onto the actor bringing forth a speech-suppressive claim would protect public access to information and expression, and in turn, individual and collective self-determination.

A shift in burden of proof would restore fair use's codified goal to define the scope of exclusive rights held by copyright holders under § 107 of the Copyright Act, entitled "Limitations on exclusive rights: fair use."[170] In its current form, however, fair use appears to *expand* the scope of exclusive rights. Ned Snow phrases the procedural aspect of the proposal eloquently:

> A copyright holder's general burden of demonstrating that a defendant's use falls within the scope of the holder's rights should require the copyright holder to demonstrate that the defendant's use is not fair. To prevail on any claim of infringement, a copyright holder should be required to prove the absence of fair use, or in other words, to prove that the use is unfair. Fair use, then, should be a right of expression that competes with copyright's right of exclusion.[169]

---

[167] *See* Philadelphia Newspaper, Inc. v. Hepps, 475 U.S. 767, 777 (1986) (holding that the burden of proof in a libel action must be placed with the private-figure plaintiff in matters of public concern).

[168] *See Proving Fair Use*, *supra* note 36, at 1797; 17 U.S.C. § 107.

[169] *Proving Fair Use*, *supra* note 36, at 1807–08.

Indeed, shifting the burden of proof onto copyright holders would result in more courts recognizing that the fair-use expression should—from both a legal and normative perspective—receive relatively more protection than copyrighted expression. This is an especially salient point when considering the evidentiary problems that plague fair users today. Put simply, fair use should be treated as a right of expression rather than a limited exception to copyright, and shifting the burden of proof is a major step in that direction.

I. CONCLUSION

Many modern-day critical modes of expression that have emerged from the proliferation of digital technologies do not fall within the traditional bounds of the fair-use standard. Yet, fair use is one of the most vital legal mechanisms, as it is charged with reconciling the Free Speech Clause with the Copyright Clause. Today, the way courts apply fair use is increasingly unsuited to appraise the cultural value of internet-era, often heterodox, collage and appropriation forms of art. The uncertainty alone from fair-use jurisprudence severely chills critical expression. Therefore, the doctrinal and procedural proposal for reform that is furnished in this essay will aid in realigning fair use with contemporary expressive activity as well as protect the high-order set of conditions that nurture the hallmarks of cultural democracy—that is, individual self-determination and equal access to participation in cultural meaning-making through critical expression. An updated, re-conceptualized fair use will once again act as a mechanism that harmonizes free speech and copyright, and safeguard the free and widespread dissemination of expression and ideas.

ANGLING FOR JUSTICE: USING FEDERAL LAW TO REEL IN CATFISHING

*Mandi Cohen**

The term "catfishing" describes the phenomenon of internet predators fabricating their identities and social circles online to trick people into romantic or emotional relationships. Although a handful of state legislatures have attempted to address catfishing in recent years, this form of predation persists and continues to evolve. This Article demonstrates that the law has not yet adequately addressed the catfishing phenomenon. Currently, catfishing laws vary by state and are often either non-existent, incomplete, or ineffective. As a result, catfish predators are not sufficiently deterred or punished, and victims of catfishing are not obtaining adequate redress. This Article thus proposes a uniform solution to address catfishing: a federal anti-catfishing statute. The proposed federal statute will deter and punish catfish predators more effectively than the current legal framework, while also providing redress to catfishing victims.

* J.D., 2018, Florida State University, College of Law.

TABLE OF CONTENTS

I. INTRODUCTION

You have been dating Stacey for several months now. She is great—smart, kind, educated, and not to mention, beautiful. You both have so much in common, from your mutual love for animals to both being single parents. You even share the same favorite movie: Alfred Hitchcock's *Psycho*. Stacey is a horror-movie fanatic, just like you. Stacey gets you, and you have not felt that way in a long time.

Stacey is more free-spirited than you, which you love. She encourages you to have fun and take risks. She was the one who encouraged you to apply for that promotion you got last month—the one you never would have had the guts to apply for if not for Stacey. Stacey frequently struggles with money, though, which is understandable because she is a single mom. Stacey's husband died in a terrible car crash a few years ago, and she has struggled financially ever since.

Overall, you see a real future with Stacey. Although you have never been married, you have a seven-year-old daughter named Marla, and you want her to finally have a real family. Stacey seems to be a great mother to her daughter, and you think she would be a great mother and role model for Marla, too. You have fallen head over heels for this woman and cannot wait to marry her. There's only one problem: you have never met her. Well, at least not in person.

You met Stacey on Facebook last year around Thanksgiving. She sent you a friend request, which you accepted because you thought she was attractive. You had a few mutual friends and figured you and her could "hook up." After all, this wouldn't be the first time you hooked up with a girl from Facebook—you and your friends used to do it often. Stacey was different, though. She had a *Psycho* movie cover on her page, which immediately intrigued you. And you two hit it off right away when she messaged you to say hello. In fact, you two have talked every day by phone and text since then.

But do you *really* know Stacey? What if you found out that Stacey is really an older, overweight woman who stole an Instagram model's photos to create a fake identity online? Or what if she is really a man? What if Stacey is really one of your friends who knows a lot about you, like your love for *Psycho* and that you used to pick girls up on Facebook? What then?

The term "catfishing" is used to describe the practice of internet predators fabricating their online identities and social circles to trick people into romantic or emotional relationships.[1] There are often two or more victims in a catfishing scheme: (1) the person, or people, whose photo or likeness is used, without his or her consent, to create the false identity on social media; and (2) the person, or people, tricked into a romantic or emotional relationship with the catfish predator based on the false social media identity.[2] The problem, however, is that the law has not yet adequately addressed catfishing or its substantial harms. This Article therefore proposes a legal framework to address catfishing.

Part II of this Article works to define catfishing and its harms through an exploration of the origin of the term "catfish" and various real-world instances of catfishing. Part III then lays out the current legal framework in the United States to address catfishing, surveying the common law, state law, and any applicable federal law. Part IV also explains why the existing legal framework ineffectively addresses catfishing and its harms. Finally, Part V examines alternatives to the existing framework. Part V ultimately argues that the most effective solution to deter and punish catfish predators is the enactment of a federal statute designed specifically to address catfishing and like harms. The proposed federal statute would also provide adequate redress for both types of catfishing victims.

II. CATFISHING & ITS ORIGIN

In 2007, Nev Schulman, a New York City photographer, was contacted by a young girl on Myspace asking permission to paint one of

---

[1] Zimmerman v. Bd. of Trs. of Ball State Univ., 940 F. Supp. 2d 875, 891 (S.D. Ind. 2013) (defining "catfishing" as "the phenomenon of internet predators that fabricate their online identities and entire social circles to trick people into emotional/romantic relationships (over a long period of time).").

[2] *Cf.* Olivia Waring, *What is catfishing and how can you spot it?*, METRO (Mar. 18, 2018), https://metro.co.uk/2018/03/18/catfishing-can-spot-7396549/ (defining catfishing as "the act of pretending to be someone you are not online, in order to lure someone you've never met into a relationship.").

his photographs.[3] Soon after, Nev received numerous packages with the girl's drawings and paintings.[4] Nev's brother and friend, who both happened to be filmmakers, decided to start filming the story.[5]

During the next couple of months, Nev became Facebook friends with members of the young girl's friends and family, including the girl's adult sister, Megan.[6] Nev and Megan had a lot in common, and Nev was physically attracted to Megan—she was a beautiful and talented singer.[7] The two developed a romantic relationship over the next several months, but they never met in person. [8] Still, Nev could not wait to start a new life with Megan.[9]

Everything came crashing down when Nev learned that Megan's lyrics and vocal recordings were actually sourced from the internet and not performed by Megan herself.[10] Nev, with his brother and friend, decided to travel to Michigan to find out the truth.[11] But unfortunately for Nev, the truth was that Megan was fake—Nev was really talking to a homebound, married woman named Angela who had made it all up.[12] Luckily for

---

[3] Thomas Berman and Rebecca Mulford, *Inside 'Catfish': A Tale of Twisted Cyber Romance*, ABC NEWS (Oct. 8, 2010), http://abcnews.go.com/2020/catfish-movie-tale-twisted-cyber-romance/story?id=11817470.

[4] *Id.*

[5] *Id.*

[6] *Id.*

[7] *Id.*

[8] *Id.*

[9] *Id.*

[10] *Id.*

[11] *Id.*

[12] CATFISH (Relativity Media and Rogue Pictures 2010).

viewers, the whole story was caught on film and was released in 2010 as a documentary entitled *Catfish.*[13]

Since the film, the term "catfishing" has been used to describe internet predators who fabricate their identities and social circles online to trick people into romantic or emotional relationships.[14] Nev's website also defines the term "cat-fish" as "a person who pretends to be someone they're not, using social media to create a false identity, particularly to pursue deceitful online romances."[15] And in 2014, "Catfish" was officially added to the Merriam-Webster Dictionary, featuring a definition similar to Nev's:

> **Catfish** (noun): a person who sets up a false personal profile on a social networking site for fraudulent or deceptive purposes.[16]

The television channel MTV even decided to hire Nev to host a reality show entitled *Catfish: the TV Show*.[17] Like the *Catfish* documentary, *Catfish: the TV Show* brings couples together who have met online but have never met in person—posing the question: "What will happen when they meet in real life for the first time?"[18] As it turns out, the answer is usually that someone was a victim of catfishing. MTV recently aired its seventh season of the show.[19]

---

[13] *Id.*

[14] *See* Zimmerman v. Bd. of Trs. of Ball State Univ., 940 F. Supp. 2d 875, 891 (S.D. Ind. 2013) (quoting URBAN DICTIONARY).

[15] Nev Schulman, *Catfish*, Nevshulman.com, http://www.nevschulman.com/catfish/ (last visited Oct. 09, 2017).

[16] *Catfish*, MERRIAM-WEBSTER ONLINE, https://www.merriam-webster.com/dictionary/catfish?utm_campaign=sd&utm_medium=serp&utm_source=jsonld (last updated Oct. 11, 2018).

[17] *Catfish: The TV Show*, MTV (Aug. 08, 2018), http://www.mtv.com/shows/catfish-the-tv-show (last visited Aug. 8, 2018).

[18] *Id.*

[19] *Id.*

I. WHAT'S THE HARM?

While it may make for entertaining reality television, catfishing causes real harms. Two or more people are often victims in a catfishing scheme: (1) the person, or people, whose photo or likeness the catfish predator uses; and (2) the person, or people, tricked into a relationship with the catfish predator. Both types of victims may suffer substantial harm from being catfished. The victim whose photo or likeness is used by the catfish predator may suffer damages to her reputation, for instance. While the victim tricked into a relationship with the catfish predator may suffer from emotional distress and financial loss.

The scope of catfishing may continue to expand as more and more people use and rely on social media to meet people and develop relationships. In a 2012 U.S. Securities and Exchange Commission quarterly report, Facebook reported that 1.5% of its 950 million monthly active users (14.25 million) were classified as "undesirable accounts."[20] An undesirable account, according to Facebook, is a user profile used for purposes that violate Facebook's terms of service (such as pretending to be someone that you are not).[21] Today, Facebook reports it has 2.23 billion monthly active users—more than double that of 2012.[22] Facebook also reports that fake accounts represent about 3–4% (66–89.2 million) of those users.[23]

There have been many high-profile stories of catfishing in the past few years, including those of Megan Meier and Chris "Birdman" Anderson. These stories help further define catfishing and illustrate various types of harm caused by the phenomenon.

---

[20] Facebook, Inc., Quarterly Report (Form 10-Q), at 24 (July 31, 2012).

[21] *Id.*

[22] FACEBOOK, *Company Info*, https://newsroom.fb.com/company-info/ (last visited Nov. 2, 2018).

[23] Guy Rosen, *Facebook Publishes Enforcement Numbers for the First Time*, FACEBOOK (May 15, 2018), https://newsroom.fb.com/news/2018/05/enforcement-numbers/.

a. The Harm to Megan Meier

In 2006, Megan Meier was a 13-year-old girl who had struggled with her weight, self-esteem, and depression for most of her life.[24] But then she met Josh Evans, a cute 16-year-old boy on Myspace, who thought she was pretty.[25] During the next few weeks, Megan, under the supervision of her mother, developed a relationship with Josh.[26] She did not meet Josh in person or even talk to him on the phone, but she talked to him regularly online.[27]

Shortly before Megan's fourteenth birthday, Josh's messages to Megan took a turn. Josh started accusing Megan of being mean to her friends, and stated that he was not sure whether he wanted to be friends with her anymore.[28] On the day Megan had handed out invitations for her birthday party at school, the arguments with Josh came to a head.[29] Josh had shared some of his and Megan's private messages with others, causing kids to say mean things about Megan—like that she was a slut and was fat.[30] In a final message to Megan, Josh told her that she was a bad person, that everyone hated her, and that the world would be a better place without her.[31] Later that day, thirteen-year-old Megan hanged herself in her closet.[32]

---

[24] Steve Pokin, *The Story of Megan Meir's Suicide*, SPRINGFIELD NEWS-LEADER: POKIN AROUND (Nov. 19, 2014), http://www.news-leader.com/story/life/2014/11/19/pokin-around-biggest-story-young-girls-suicide/19291825/ [hereinafter Pokin].

[25] MEGAN MEIER FOUNDATION, *Megan's Story*, (Nov. 13, 2007), https://www.meganmeierfoundation.org/megans-story.html [hereinafter MEGAN MEIER FOUNDATION].

[26] *Id.*

[27] *Id.*

[28] *Id.*

[29] *Id.*

[30] *Id.*

[31] *Id.*

[32] *Id.*

Six weeks after the passing of their daughter, Megan's parents learned that Josh never existed.[33] Megan had been catfished, even while under her mother's supervision. The Myspace profile was created by a long-time friend and neighbor of the Meiers, Lori Drew.[34] Drew created the profile to find out what Megan was saying online about her daughter, Sarah.[35] To create the profile, Drew posted a photo of a young boy, without his consent, to attract Megan.[36] Drew also used the intimate details she knew about Megan's struggle with her weight, self-esteem, and depression to bully Megan.[37]

Even under the supervision of her parents, Megan Meier was duped into a romantic relationship online. She was purposefully tormented and bullied, which ultimately led to such great emotional distress that she took her own life. The Megan Meier story reveals the extent of emotional harm a victim may experience from a catfishing scheme. It also demonstrates how malicious behavior, like bullying, may accompany catfishing.

b. The Harm to Chris "Birdman" Anderson

In 2011, Chris "Birdman" Anderson was a 33-year-old professional basketball player for the Denver Nuggets.[38] Paris Dunn was a 17-year-old Instagram model who enjoyed flirting with pro-athletes online (she often lied about her age).[39] One day, Dunn got a Facebook message, supposedly

---

[33] *Id.*

[34] *See* Pokin, *supra* note 24.

[35] *Id.*

[36] United States v. Drew, 259 F.R.D. 449, 452 (C.D. Cal. 2009).

[37] MEGAN MEIER FOUNDATION, *supra* note 25.

[38] Andrew Paparella et. al., *How NBA Star, Aspiring Model Became Victims of a Massive Catfishing Scheme Out of Canada*, ABC NEWS (April 13, 2017), http://abcnews.go.com/Technology/nba-star-aspiring-model-victims-massive-catfishing-scheme/story?id=46755887.

[39] *Id.*

from Birdman, and the two hit it off.[40] They started emailing, texting, and exchanging pictures (including nude pictures).[41] They even shared a weekend together—in person at Birdman's house in Colorado.[42] But the relationship turned out to be part of a catfishing scheme. And the consequences to Birdman and Dunn were tremendous.

Unbeknownst to Dunn and Birdman, the relationship and in-person meeting had been orchestrated by a catfish predator, Shelly Chartier—an isolated Canadian woman who impersonated both Birdman and Dunn.[43] Months later, in 2012, Birdman got an email from Chartier, claiming to be Dunn's mother demanding money from Birdman.[44] The email revealed that Dunn was under the age of eighteen at the time she and Birdman spent the weekend and exchanged nude photos.[45] The nude photos of Dunn on Birdman's phone were thus considered child pornography.[46] Birdman's attorney sent money to the drafter of the email in an effort to make the issue go away.[47] It did not work. Birdman was ultimately investigated by police, who seized his computers, phones, and other electronic devices.[48] The story became public, and Birdman was let go from the Nuggets at the end of the season.[49]

Meanwhile, Dunn was receiving messages from Chartier, claiming to be a friend of Birdman, and threatening to have Dunn raped and

---

[40] *Id.*

[41] *Id.*

[42] *Id.*

[43] *Id.*

[44] *Id.*

[45] *Id.*

[46] *Id.*

[47] *Id.*

[48] *Id.*

[49] *Id.*

murdered.[50] The friend also threatened to post Dunn's nude photos, name, address, and phone number online because Dunn mentioned being invited to meet a different basketball star.[51] Dunn's nude photos ended up being posted online for a short period of time.[52]

The Birdman story illustrates how complex and harmful a catfishing scheme can be. Almost unbelievably, both victims in this story actually met in person and still did not realize they were the prey of a sophisticated catfish predator. Nev Shulman called the scheme "one of the most complicated, confusing" cases he had ever seen.[53] Chartier received money from Birdman's attorney, publicly embarrassed Birdman, caused him to be formally investigated for child pornography, and caused him to lose his job with the NBA.[54] Dunn also suffered substantial emotional distress, and had her nude pictures posted online.[55]

The harms caused by catfishing are real. Victims of catfishing, both those who are impersonated and those who are tricked into a relationship, may suffer from a variety of financial, social, and emotional harms as a result of catfishing. And as discussed above, the scope of the catfishing problem may continue to grow with the increasing reliance on social media. It is therefore important that the law address the catfishing phenomenon. Ideally, regimes would discourage and punish catfishing. As Part II explains, however, current laws are insufficient to address the challenges catfishing poses.

V. The Current Legal Framework

There are various common-law, state-law, and federal-law mechanisms in place that deal with catfishing. However, the existing

---

[50] *Id.*

[51] *Id.*

[52] *Id.*

[53] *Id.*

[54] *Id.*

[55] *Id.*

framework provides a piecemeal, and often inadequate, set of remedies to victims. Furthermore, the existing framework has been insufficient to deter or punish catfish predators. The following sections survey the current legal framework, illustrating how it has been ineffective in fully addressing catfishing and its harms.

a. The Common-Law Framework

Various common-law tort claims exist that may be used to address catfishing in limited instances. These claims include misappropriation of likeness, fraud, and intentional infliction of emotional distress.

i. Misappropriation of Likeness

In a catfishing scheme, the victim whose photo or likeness was used without consent could theoretically sue the catfish predator for misappropriation of likeness. The Restatement (Second) of Torts states: "One who appropriates to his own use or benefit the name or likeness of another is subject to liability to the other for invasion of his privacy."[56] While it is conceivable that a misappropriation-of-likeness claim could be brought in a catfishing case, courts have not yet extended the claim to social media.[57] Furthermore, the Restatement acknowledges that the claim varies by state, and that some states generally do not allow misappropriation-of-likeness claims unless there is a showing of commercial use or benefit.[58] Commercial settings involve promotional activities, such as advertising, which are not typically associated with catfishing.[59] So regardless of whether the claim is extended to social media, most catfishing victims would be unable to bring the claim in certain states because of catfishing's noncommercial nature.

---

[56] RESTATEMENT (SECOND) OF TORTS § 652C (AM. LAW INST. 1979).

[57] Bradley D. Kay, Note, *Extending Tort Liability to Creators of Fake Profiles on Social Networking Websites*, 10 CHI-KENT J. INTELL. PROP. 1, 13–14 (2010).

[58] *Id.*

[59] *Using the Name or Likeness of Another*, DIGITAL MEDIA L. PROJECT, http://www.dmlp.org/legal-guide/using-name-or-likeness-another (last visited Dec. 15, 2017).

ii. Fraudulent Misrepresentation

If the victim of a catfishing scheme sent money to the catfish predator, the victim could conceivably make a fraudulent-misrepresentation claim against the catfish predator. The Restatement (Second) of Torts states:

> One who fraudulently makes a misrepresentation of fact, opinion, intention, or law for the purpose of inducing another to act or to refrain from action in reliance upon it, is subject to liability to the other in deceit for pecuniary loss caused to him by his justifiable reliance upon the misrepresentation.[60]

Based on a plain language reading of the Restatement, a catfish predator may be liable for fraudulent misrepresentation if the catfish predator purposely lies to his or her victim to get money. However, courts have generally held this not to be the case.[61]

In *Bonhomme v. St. James*,[62] for instance, an Illinois court held that a victim of a catfish scheme was unable to recover the money she gave her catfish predator.[63] The victim, Paula Bonhomme, was targeted by a female catfish predator pretending to be a man named Jesse.[64] The two communicated online and by telephone (the catfish predator used a device to disguise her voice as a male voice during the calls).[65] The catfish predator created approximately twenty fictional identities to be involved

---

[60] RESTATEMENT (SECOND) OF TORTS § 525 (AM. LAW INST. 1979).

[61] KENNETH W. CLARKSON ET AL., BUSINESS LAW: TEXT AND CASES 299 (13th ed. 2014).

[62] 970 N.E.2d 1 (Ill. 2012).

[63] *Id.* at 11–12.

[64] *Id.* at 3–4.

[65] *Id.* at 4.

with "Jesse."[66] Over the course of the relationship, Bonhomme sent over $10,000 to these fictional people.[67]

Although Bonhomme incurred significant financial loss because of the catfishing scheme, the court denied her relief, reasoning that the relationship between the parties was a purely personal relationship:

> Plaintiff and defendant were not engaged in any kind of business dealings or bargaining, and the veracity of representations made in the context of purely private personal relationships is simply not something the state regulates or in which the state processes any kind of valid public policy interest. Consequently, as regrettable as the alleged facts are, we hold that they are not the types of facts upon which a claim for fraudulent misrepresentation may be held.[68]

Thus, while it would appear from the Restatement's plain language that victims may be able to recover from the financial loss suffered from a catfishing scheme, courts generally require more than a purely personal relationship to bring a claim.[69]

iii. Intentional Infliction of Emotional Distress

Catfishing victims may also consider suing their catfish predators for intentional infliction of emotional distress, especially when the catfish predator makes no financial gain. However, plaintiffs must meet a high bar to succeed on a claim of intentional infliction of emotional distress (IIED).[70]

---

[66] *Id.* at 5.

[67] *Id.*

[68] *Id.* at 26–27.

[69] CLARKSON, *supra* note 60, at 299.

[70] *See generally* RESTATEMENT (SECOND) OF TORTS § 46 (AM. LAW INST. 1979) ("The liability clearly does not extend to mere insults, indignities, threats, annoyances, petty

The Restatement (Second) of Torts states: "One who by extreme and outrageous conduct intentionally or recklessly causes severe emotional distress to another is subject to liability for such emotional distress, and if bodily harm to the other results from it, for such bodily harm."[71] The Restatement goes on to explain the high extreme-and-outrageous standard, stating that the conduct must "go beyond all possible bounds of decency, and to be regarded as atrocious, and utterly intolerable in a civilized community."[72]

It may seem clear that the behavior described in Megan Meier's story,[73] for instance, would qualify as "extreme and outrageous."[74] However, case law suggests otherwise. In *Draker v. Schrieber*,[75] the court found that the vice-principal of a Texas high school was unable to recover for IIED when students created a fake Myspace profile of her that included her picture and employment information, as well as graphic and sexual references about her.[76] The concurring opinion in the case discussed the Meier story, as well as other similar tragic stories, to highlight how high the bar is to establish the extreme-and-outrageous-conduct element of an IIED claim:

---

oppressions, or other trivialities. . . . There is no occasion for the law to intervene in every case where someone's feeling are hurt.").

[71] *Id.*

[72] *Id.* § 46 cmt. d.

[73] *See, e.g.*, United States v. Drew, 259 F.R.D. 449, 452 (C.D. Cal. 2009) (illustrating an adult using the intimate details she knew about a child's low self-esteem and depression to torment her online using a fake profile).

[74] *See, e.g.*, Doe v. Hofstetter, No. 11-cv-02209-DME-MJW, 2012 U.S. Dist. LEXIS 82320, at *19–22 (D. Colo. June 13, 2012) (finding that a defendant's posting of a couple's intimate photos online, emailing the couple the intimate photos to harass them, and impersonating the wife on Twitter met the extreme-and-outrageous standard for an IIED claim).

[75] 271 S.W.3d 318 (Tex. App.—San Antonio 2008, no pet.).

[76] *Id.* at 325.

> There appears to be little civil remedy for the injured targets of these internet communications. Intentional infliction of emotional distress would seem to be one option. But as it has developed, the tort is nearly impossible to establish. The citizens of Texas would be better served by a fair and workable framework in which to present their claims, or by an honest statement that there is, in fact, no remedy for their damages.[77]

iv. *The Problem with Common-Law Claims*

As discussed above, there are various common-law claims that could apply to catfishing. But as we have seen, only in limited circumstances would a catfishing victim even able to bring suit. For a misappropriation-of-likeness claim, commercial use of a victim's photo or likeness is required to sue in certain states.[78] This requirement will bar recovery in many cases in which the relationship is noncommercial in nature.[79] Furthermore, a misappropriation-of-likeness claim could provide redress to only one of the two types of catfishing victims.[80] For a catfishing victim who provided money to the catfish predator, a fraudulent-misrepresentation claim is conceivable.[81] Yet some courts have ruled that catfishing schemes are purely personal and therefore do not qualify for the claim.[82] Finally, victims can bring IIED claims against catfish predators, but only where a catfish predator's conduct is so extreme and outrageous

---

[77] *Id.* at 327 (Stone, J., concurring).

[78] RESTATEMENT (SECOND) OF TORTS § 652C cmt. b (AM. LAW INST. 1979).

[79] *See id.* ("Statutes in some states have, however, limited the liability to commercial uses of the name or likeness.")

[80] Only the victim whose photo/likeness was used would be able to bring misappropriation of likeness claim. The victim who was tricked by the catfish predator's use of the photo/likeness cannot make such a claim.

[81] The Better Business Bureau alone received over 50 reports of catfishing, resulting in over $500,000 of losses, in years 2015–2016. *Don't get hooked by a catfish scam*, BBB (June 23, 2017), https://www.bbb.org/central-texas/news-events/news-releases/2016/06/dont-get-hooked-by-a-catfish-scam/.

[82] *E.g.*, Bonhomme v. St. James, 970 N.E.2d 1, 10–11 (Ill. 2012).

as to "go beyond all possible bounds of decency, and to be regarded as atrocious, and utterly intolerable in a civilized community."[83] This is a high standard to meet, and courts have acknowledged that even a case as extreme as the Megan Meier's story will not prevail on this claim.[84]

Even assuming a victim had a potentially viable tort claim against a catfish predator, litigation is expensive.[85] The ambiguity of whether a common-law claim would be viable, combined with the cost of litigation, may deter many victims of catfishing from pursuing a lawsuit. Catfish predators may also be judgment-proof, potentially leaving even those victims successful with common-law claims without adequate redress.

b. State Statutes

In some states, like New Jersey, it is a criminal offense for a catfish predator to use someone's photo or likeness without consent to create fake social-media identities.[86] Other states like Oklahoma have adopted legislation allowing for civil recovery in these cases.[87] California has adopted a statute that exposes catfish predators to both criminal and civil liability.[88] But a majority of states still lack legislation expressly aimed at addressing the catfishing phenomenon.[89] An evident shortcoming of relying on state legislation is that there is great variation in the handling of

---

83 RESTATEMENT (SECOND) OF TORTS § 46 cmt. a (AM. LAW INST. 1979).

84 *Cf. Drew*, 259 F.R.D. at 452–53 (mentioning intentional infliction of emotional distress and ultimately dismissing the criminal charges).

85 Robert Bovarnick, *When is Litigation Worth the Hassle?*, FORBES (July 21, 2010), https://www.forbes.com/2010/07/21/when-to-sue-entrepreneurs-law-taxation-bovarnick.html.

86 N.J. STAT. § 2C:21-17 (2017); TEX. PEN. CODE ANN. § 33.07 (2017).

87 OKLA. STAT. tit. 12, § 1450 (2017).

88 CAL. PENAL CODE § 528.5 (2017).

89 Reputation Defender, *Online Impersonation Laws*, (Aug. 17, 2012), https://www.reputationdefender.com/blog/privacy/online-impersonation-laws [hereinafter Reputation Defender].

catfishing among the states. Still, a survey of current state legislation may help identify a more effective framework.

i. New Jersey

In New Jersey, it is a crime to use electronic communications, an internet website, or other means to "impersonate[] another or assume[] a false identity and does an act in such assumed character or false identity for the purpose of obtaining a benefit for himself or another or to injure or defraud another."[90] According to New Jersey's statute, "benefit" includes any property, pecuniary amount, services, or "any injury or harm perpetrated on another where there is no pecuniary value." [91]

New Jersey's statute is broad enough to cover both catfishing and identity theft in general.[92] And both impersonation of an actual person and creation of a false identity are outlawed.[93] However, while the statute outlines criminal penalties for violation, no civil remedies for the victims of such violation are expressly provided in the statute.[94]

ii. Oklahoma

Oklahoma recently adopted legislation that allows for civil recovery for catfishing: the "Catfishing Liability Act."[95] The Act provides:

> "Any person who knowingly uses another's name, voice, signature, photograph or likeness through social media to

[90] N.J. STAT. § 2C:21–17.

[91] *Id.*

[92] New Jersey State Police, *Identity Theft* http://www.njsp.org/tech/identity.html#pit. (last visited Oct. 9, 2017).

[93] N.J. STAT. § 2C:21–17.

[94] *Id.*

[95] Sara Morrison, *New Anti-Catfishing Law is the Toughest in the US*, VOCATIV (May 17, 2016), http://www.vocativ.com/319357/new-anti-catfishing-law-is-the-toughest-in-the-us/index.html [hereinafter Morrison].

> create a false identity without such person's consent . . . for the purpose of harming, intimidating, threatening or defrauding such person shall be liable for online impersonation and liable for any damages sustained by the person or persons injured as a result thereof . . . ."[96]

The Act has been called the "toughest" in the nation, and it took effect in November 2016.[97]

Unlike the New Jersey statute, which is comprehensive enough to cover both catfishing and identity theft in the broader sense, Oklahoma's statute specifically targets catfishing. The statute also includes various clauses limiting the scope of the statute, which will help prevent First Amendment challenges and conflicts with other laws. Specifically, the statute excludes liability when the sole purpose of the online impersonation is satire or parody.[98] The statute also excludes liability to law enforcement investigating internet crime.[99] Finally, the statute recognizes that federal law provides social media companies immunity from liability for catfishing acts perpetrated by their users, and reaffirms that no such liability should be construed from the statute.[100]

Oklahoma's statute provides catfishing victims the opportunity for injunctive relief and damages (including punitive damages).[101] Attorney's fees may also be awarded under the statute, and the statute states that all remedies are cumulative and in addition to any others provided for by law.[102]

---

[96] OKLA. STAT. tit. 12, § 1450 (2017).

[97] Morrison, *supra* note 94.

[98] OKLA. STAT. tit. 12, § 1450 (2017).

[99] *Id.*

[100] *Id.*

[101] *Id.*

[102] *Id.*

Overall, Oklahoma's statute is appealing—it provides a civil claim to anyone defrauded or otherwise harmed by catfishing. However, the statute is limited to impersonation of an actual person (compared to New Jersey's statute, which includes both impersonation and creating a fake identity). The statute is also narrowly limited to social media,[103] which may limit its ability to keep up with evolving technology. Finally, while the statute is intended to provide a civil remedy to catfishing victims, this goal may not always come to fruition (e.g., in cases where a catfish predator is judgment-proof). Providing criminal penalties in addition to a civil remedy would be more comprehensive in deterring and punishing catfishing predators.

iii. California

California's statute imposes both civil and criminal liability for online impersonation.[104] The statute provides that "any person who knowingly and without consent credibly impersonates another actual person through or on an Internet web site or by other electronic means for purposes of harming, intimidating, threatening, or defrauding another person is guilty of a public offense . . . ."[105] The statute goes on to say that "[i]n addition to any other civil remedy available, a person who suffers damage or loss by reason of a violation [of the statute] may bring a civil action against the violator for compensatory damages and injunctive relief or other equitable relief . . . ."[106]

This combination of civil and criminal liability effectively deters and punishes catfishing, while providing redress to victims. For instance, if a catfish predator is judgment-proof when held liable under the civil portion of the statute, he may still be punished under the criminal portion of the statute. Also, the combination of criminal and civil liability promotes the seriousness of the offense to hopefully deter catfishing.

---

[103] *Id.* (defining social media as "forms of electronic communication through which users create online communities to share information, ideas, personal messages, and other content").

[104] CAL. PENAL CODE § 528.5.

[105] *Id.*

[106] *Id.*

California's statute is broad enough to cover internet websites and other electronic communications, unlike Oklahoma's statute, which is limited to social media.[107] Still, because California's statute is limited to impersonation of actual persons (unlike New Jersey's statute that also covers creating fake profiles), certain victims of catfishing may be left without recourse.[108]

iv. The Problem with State Statutes

Each of the state statutes surveyed in this part of the Article has advantages and disadvantages. For instance, New Jersey's statute is not limited to impersonation of an actual person, but it does not expressly provide for civil remedies to catfishing victims.[109] Oklahoma's statute provides a variety of potential civil remedies for catfishing victims, but it does not criminalize the offense to ensure punishment even where a catfish predator is judgment-proof for civil purposes.[110] California's statute includes both civil and criminal liability for catfish predators, but the statute's scope is limited to impersonation of an actual person.[111]

There is little uniformity among existing state anti-catfishing statutes, and most states still completely lack statutes aimed to address catfishing.[112] Also, given the interstate nature of the internet,[113] jurisdictional issues may also arise with state statutes. A well-crafted state statute may sufficiently address cases in which the catfish predator is in the

---

[107] *Id.*; OKLA. STAT. tit. 12, § 1450 (2017).

[108] CAL. PENAL CODE § 528.5 (2017); N.J. STAT. § 2C:21–17.

[109] N.J. STAT. § 2C:21–17.

[110] OKLA. STAT. tit. 12, § 1450 (2017).

[111] CAL. PENAL CODE § 528.5.

[112] Reputation Defender, *supra* note 89.

[113] *See* South Dakota v. Wayfair, Inc., 138 S.Ct. 2080, 2097 (2018) (noting that the internet has "changed the dynamics of the national economy" and "interstate marketplace").

same state as her victims.[114] However, in cases spanning across multiple states, it may be difficult to obtain jurisdiction over a catfish predator or determine which state's statute should apply.[115] Therefore, catfishing is more appropriately addressed at the federal level.

c. Federal Statutes

Given the interstate nature of the internet, and the uniformity and jurisdictional issues at the state level,[116] catfishing is likely best addressed by federal law. Currently, the United States lacks a federal statute specifically designed to address catfishing. There are a few statutes related to the ideas and harms behind catfishing that may apply in limited circumstances, though. These statutes include the Interstate Communications Act,[117] the Interstate Stalking Act,[118] the Stored Communications Act,[119] and the Computer Fraud and Abuse Act.[120]

i. The Interstate Communications Act

The Interstate Communications Act criminalizes the transmission of certain communications in interstate or foreign commerce.[121] The purpose of the Act is to prohibit extortion through interstate communications.[122] The Act largely deals with ransom demands for kidnapped persons and extortion attempts by threatening to kidnap a

---

[114] *See, e.g.,* Megan Meier Foundation, *supra* note 25 (where the catfish predator was a neighbor).

[115] Stephanie K. Marshall, et al., *Conflict of Laws*, 62 SMU L. REV. 1021, 1025–26 (2009).

[116] *See Wayfair, Inc.*, 138 S.Ct. at 2086.

[117] 18 U.S.C. § 875 (1994).

[118] 18 U.S.C. § 2261A (2013).

[119] 18 U.S.C. § 2701 (2002).

[120] 18 U.S.C. § 1030 (2008).

[121] 18 U.S.C. § 875 (1994).

[122] United States v. Cooper, 523 F.2d 8, 10 (6th Cir. 1975).

person.[123] The fourth section of the Act, however, outlaws interstate transmission of communications containing threats to injure the reputation of a person, with intent to extort any money or other things of value.[124]

In *United States v. Petrovic*,[125] the defendant made threats to post pornographic video and images of his ex-wife if she ended their relationship.[126] The defendant carried out the threats by creating a website containing the pornographic content, along with personal information about his ex-wife. The defendant mailed postcards to her family, friends, and community contacts, inviting them to view the website.[127] He demanded his ex-wife continue their relationship or pay him $100,000 to take the website down.[128] The court in *Petrovic* found that a sexual relationship may be an intangible "thing of value" that a person may intend to extort.[129] The court thus affirmed the defendant's conviction under the statute.[130]

Given the *Petrovic* holding, catfish predators who make threats to injure the reputation of their victim, to extort money or a continued sexual relationship with the victim, may face liability under 18 U.S.C. § 875. It is important to note, though, that *Petrovic* involved a previously married couple that had physically met and engaged in an in-person sexual relationship, which is unlikely in most catfishing situations. Also, *Petrovic* involved extortion for money and the continuance of the in-person sexual relationship. Section 875 may therefore be most useful in extreme catfishing cases like the Birdman case, which involved an in-person

---

[123] 18 U.S.C. § 875 (2017).

[124] *Id.*

[125] 701 F.3d 849 (8th Cir. 2012).

[126] *Id.* at 852–53.

[127] *Id.*

[128] *Id.*

[129] *Id.* at 858.

[130] *Id.* at 860.

encounter, extortion for money from Birdman, and extortion for a continued relationship with Dunn (or least to prevent her from entering a new relationship with a different basketball star).

ii. The Interstate Stalking Act

Under the Interstate Stalking Act, a person who uses electronic communication services or systems of interstate commerce with "intent to kill, injure, harass, or intimidate" another person is criminally liable if the conduct puts the victim in reasonable fear of serious bodily injury or if the conduct would reasonably be expected to cause the victim substantial emotional distress.[131]

In addition to being convicted under 18 U.S.C. § 875, the defendant in *Petrovic* was also convicted under this federal stalking statute for his threats to, and actual posting of, pornographic images and videos—both of which caused substantial emotional distress to his ex-wife.[132] There have been several convictions under this statute that have involved romantic relationships on the internet, or even more closely tied to catfishing: social media.[133] However, each of these cases involved the defendant harassing a victim with whom he shared a prior in-person relationship by posting sexual photos of the victim online. This is unlikely in most catfishing situations, because the general purpose of catfishing is to trick someone into a romantic or emotional relationship rather than harass a former lover by posting sexual pictures. Therefore, like 18 U.S.C. § 875, this statute may help criminally punish catfish predators in rare cases like the Birdman case, involving in-person sexual relations and posting of sexual photos online.

---

[131] 18 U.S.C. § 2261A (2013).

[132] *Petrovic*, 701 F.3d at 860.

[133] *See, e.g.*, United States v. Osinger, 753 F.3d 939, 947–48 (9th Cir. 2014) (convicting the defendant under 18 U.S.C. § 2261A after he created a fake Facebook profile in his ex-girlfriend's name to post explicit photos of her); United States v. Hobgood, 868 F.3d 744 (8th Cir. 2017) (convicting the defendant for making false and harmful representations to an employer of his former romantic partner).

iii. The Stored Communications Act

Section 2701 of the Stored Communications Act criminalizes intentionally accessing electronic communication services, without authorization, as well as intentionally exceeding authorization to access the electronic communication services.[134] While a plain-language reading of the statute may suggest that impersonating a person on social media would violate the statute, *Doe v. Hofstetter* made clear it would not.[135] The court in *Doe* found the statute to be an anti-hacking statute.[136] Specifically, the court was "[n]ot persuaded . . . that violating Twitter's terms of service by creating an account in Jane Doe's name qualifie[d] as 'exceed[ing] an authorization to access Twitter . . . . Defendant did not, for instance, hack into someone else's account and obtain their stored communications."[137] So unless a catfish predator hacks into a victim's account, rather than just creating a fake account, 18 U.S.C. § 2701 would not apply.

iv. The Computer Fraud and Abuse Act

The Computer Fraud and Abuse Act (CFAA) is codified as 18 U.S.C. § 1030.[138] This is the Act prosecutors used to bring changes against catfish predator Lori Drew from the Megan Meier story.[139] Among other things, the CFAA criminalizes a person who "intentionally accesses a computer without authorization or exceeds authorized access, and thereby obtains . . . information from any protected computer."[140] The Act protects computers used in interstate or foreign commerce or communication.[141]

---

[134] 18 U.S.C. § 2701 (2018).

[135] Doe v. Hofstetter, No. 11-CV-02209-DME-MJW, 2012 U.S. Dist. LEXIS 82320, at *18 (D. Colo. June 13, 2012).

[136] *Id.*

[137] *Id.*

[138] 18 U.S.C. § 1030.

[139] United States v. Drew, 259 F.R.D. 449, 456 (C.D. Cal. 2009).

[140] 18 U.S.C. § 1030(a)(2).

[141] *Id.*

The prosecutors in *Drew* argued Drew intentionally accessed a protected computer without, or in excess of, authorization when she violated the Myspace terms of service to create the fake profile she used to catfish Megan Meier.[142] The court therefore faced the question whether "intentional breach of an Internet website's terms of service, without more, is sufficient to constitute . . . violation of the CFAA."[143] The court ultimately found that interpreting the CFAA in this way would violate the two-prong void-for-vagueness doctrine, which requires notice as well as minimal guidelines for law enforcement when enforcing the Act.[144] The court found that individuals of common intelligence would not be put on notice that violating terms of service contracts could be a criminal violation of the CFAA.[145] The court also found that there would be an absence of minimal guidelines for law enforcement because it was unclear whether every intentional violation of a website's terms of service would violate CFAA.[146] Drew was therefore acquitted of her charges under the Act.[147] Given the holding in *Drew*, it is unlikely that the CFAA can be used to punish catfish predators.

v. *The Problem with the Current Federal Statutes*

Given both the uniformity and potential jurisdictional issues of state statutes aimed at catfishing, the catfishing phenomenon is likely better addressed by federal law. However, the United States currently lacks a federal statute specifically designed to address catfishing. While there are a few federal statutes related to the ideas and harms behind catfishing, none have been designed or interpreted to deter and punish catfish predators.

Courts have applied 18 U.S.C. §§ 875 and 2261A to address extortion and stalking for prior in-person relationships; for instance, where

---

[142] *Drew*, 259 F.R.D. at 457.

[143] *Id.* at 451.

[144] *Id.* at 463.

[145] *Id.* at 464.

[146] *Id.* at 466.

[147] *Id.* at 467.

someone intentionally posts sexually explicit photos of an ex-girlfriend to harass her. These statutes are therefore viable in the rare cases like the Birdman case. In comparison, 18 U.S.C. §§ 2701 and 1030 are unlikely viable at all to address most catfishing situations. Furthermore, each of these statutes focuses on the criminal prosecution of violators and do not explicitly provide civil recourse to catfishing victims. A combination of civil and criminal liability, however, would best deter and punish catfish predators and provide redress to these victims.

V. ADDRESSING THE CATFISHING PHENOMENON

Catfishing causes real harms, and the law has not yet adequately addressed them. As demonstrated in Part IV of this Article, catfishing is best addressed by federal law to ensure uniformity and to prevent potential jurisdictional issues posed by state statutes, given the interstate nature of the internet. This part of the Article explores potential federal solutions to address catfishing and ultimately argues for the most effective solution to deter and punish catfish predators: a federal anti-catfishing statute. Such a statute would also provide redress to victims of catfishing schemes.

a. Holding Social Media Companies Liable Will Not Work

One possible solution to catfishing is to hold social media companies, like Facebook, liable. This would require an amendment to 47 U.S.C. § 230 (Section 230). Currently, Section 230 provides broad immunity to "interactive computer services" for user-generated content.[148] Social media websites fall within the definition of "interactive computer services" provided in Section 230.[149]

A recently published student article suggested amending Section 230 to assign liability to social media companies when they knew, or should have known, that content was harmful.[150] The article argues that catfishing victims could then hold companies like Facebook liable when

---

[148] 47 U.S.C. § 230(f)(2) (2017).

[149] *Id.*

[150] Collen M. Koch, Comment, *To Catch a Catfish: A Statutory Solution for Victims of Online Impersonation*, 88 U. COLO. L. REV. 233, 234 (2017).

they do not remove known harmful content.[151] The article analogizes to federal copyright law as having similar provisions to hold internet service providers liable for infringement when they knew, or should have known, protected content was posted.[152]

The article's argument to amend Section 230 to hold social media companies liable for catfishing is unconvincing. Congress enacted Section 230 to grant immunity to these websites for harmful user-generated content to encourage screening and removal of such content.[153] This immunity allows social media websites leeway to screen for fake or harmful profiles. Without the full protection of Section 230, websites may choose to not screen at all for harmful content, for fear of liability. This would result in even more fake social media profiles and other harmful content being posted online. Also, amending Section 230 to hold social media companies liable for catfishing does little to deter or punish the real perpetrators involved in catfishing schemes: the catfish predators. While holding social media websites liable for catfishing may provide redress to catfishing victims, the catfish predators are left with little incentive to stop catfishing.

Congress expressly provided in Section 230 a different solution to regulating harmful content, other than holding websites liable: "Ensure vigorous enforcement of Federal criminal laws to deter and punish trafficking in obscenity, stalking, and harassment by means of computer."[154] While Congress focused on obscene content in this statement, the same could be said in the catfishing context if a federal anti-catfishing law were put in place.

b. The Most Effective Solution: A Federal Anti-Catfishing Statute

Another potential solution to the catfishing phenomenon is to hold catfish predators liable under a federal anti-catfishing statute. If structured properly, a federal anti-catfishing statute would better deter and punish

---

[151] *Id.* at 276

[152] *Id.* at 277.

[153] Kate Klonich, Article, *The New Governors: The People, Rules, and Processes Governing Online Speech*, 131 HARV. L. REV. 1598, 1602 (2017) [hereinafter Klonich].

[154] *See id.*

catfish predators than the existing piecemeal framework or than amending Section 230 to hold social media websites liable for catfishing. Such a statute would also provide adequate redress to both types of catfishing victims: (1) the person, or people, whose photo or likeness is used, without his or her consent, by a catfish predator to create a false identity on social media; and (2) the person, or people, tricked into a romantic or emotional relationship with the catfish predator based on the false social media identity.

As seen in Part IV of this Article, while state statutes to address catfishing are widely non-existent, a few states have enacted anti-catfishing statutes. Congress should therefore draw upon the strong points of these state statutes to develop and enact a uniform federal anti-catfishing statute, such as the one provided below:

Proposed United States Catfishing Liability Act.

1. As used in this Act:
    a. The term "benefit" means any property, any pecuniary amount, any services, and any pecuniary amount sought to be avoided; and
    b. The term "injure" means causing substantial harm to, including both pecuniary and non-pecuniary harm.
2. Notwithstanding any other provision of law, a person is guilty of a public offense, punishable pursuant to Section 3 of this Act, if he uses an internet website to impersonate another or assume a false identity with intent to injure, defraud, threaten, or intimidate another person, or for the purpose of fraudulently obtaining a benefit for himself or another; except where the sole purpose of the impersonation is for satire or parody.
3. A person guilty of an offense under this Act is liable to imprisonment for a term not to exceed one year, or to a fine not to exceed $1,000.00, or by both imprisonment and that fine.
4. In addition to any other civil remedy available, a person who suffers damage or loss by reason of violation of Section 2 of this Act may bring a civil suit against the violator for compensatory damages and injunctive relief or other equitable relief. Punitive damages of no less than Five Hundred Dollars ($500) per individual may be awarded to

the injured party or parties. The prevailing party in any action under this section shall be entitled to attorney fees and costs.

5. This Act does not apply to law enforcement agencies, or their employees acting within the scope of employment, while investigating crimes.
6. Nothing in this Act shall be construed to impose liability on interactive computer services, as defined in 47 U.S.C. 230, for content provided by another person.
7. This Act does not preclude prosecution under any other law. If conduct that constitutes an offense under this section also constitutes an offense under any other law, the violator may be prosecuted under this section, the other law, or both.

The federal anti-catfishing statute proposed above draws upon the strong points of currents state statutes, but because it is federal, it provides a uniform framework to enforce criminal and civil penalties for catfishing throughout the nation. This framework is also free from the potential jurisdictional issues states currently face.[155]

The proposed statute also has various other strong points. For instance, the statute makes clear that it will not inhibit police investigations or contradict Section 230 immunity for social media websites. Furthermore, the proposed statute does not limit use of other laws in conjunction with the statute. The criminal and civil components of the statute work together to promote the seriousness of the crime. Even where a catfish predator is judgment-proof from civil liability, she may still face criminal liability. Finally, both types of catfishing victims are eligible to receive compensatory, punitive, and injunctive relief under the statute (both a victim whose photo or likeness was stolen and a victim who was tricked into a relationship are eligible to bring a civil suit under the statute).

i. Constitutionality of the Proposed Federal Anti-Catfishing Statute

Like the federal statutes surveyed in Part IV, Congress would have the constitutional authority to enact the anti-catfishing statute under the

---

[155] See Part II, *supra*.

Commerce Clause, which gives Congress the ability to regulate commerce among the states.[156] "The internet is an instrumentality and channel of interstate commerce," and use of internet websites is thus within the power of Congress to regulate under the Commerce Clause.[157]

Furthermore, like the well-crafted state statutes, the federal anti-catfishing statute proposed in this Article will likely survive facial constitutional challenges. For instance, in *Ex Parte Bradshaw*, Bradshaw challenged his prosecution under Texas's online-impersonation statute.[158] Specifically, Bradshaw argued that the statute was unconstitutional on its face, violating the First, Fifth, and Fourteenth Amendments.[159] The Texas intermediate appellate court ultimately disagreed with Bradshaw in each of his arguments and upheld the constitutionality of the Texas statute.[160]

Bradshaw argued that under the First Amendment, Texas's statute was unconstitutional because it was facially overbroad.[161] There were conceivable applications of the statute that would implicate speech protected by the First Amendment.[162] Bradshaw provided examples such as comedians impersonating politicians for entertainment at the subjects' expense or to hurt the subjects' feelings.[163] The court found that the statute served a significant government interest in "protecting citizens from crime, fraud, defamation, and threats from online impersonation."[164] Further, the court found that the statute also served a "significant First Amendment interest in regulating false and compelled speech on the part of the

---

[156] U.S. CONST. art. I, § 8, cl. 3.

[157] United States v. MacEwan, 445 F.3d 237, 245 (3d Cir. 2006).

[158] Ex parte Bradshaw, 501 S.W.3d 665, 670 (Tex. App.—Dallas 2016, pet. ref'd).

[159] *Id.*

[160] *Id.* at 677–80.

[161] *Id.* at 675.

[162] *Id.*

[163] *Id.* at 675.

[164] *Id.* at 676.

individual whose identity has been appropriated."[165] The court ultimately rejected Bradshaw's First Amendment challenge because the "hypothetical" examples Bradshaw provided "fail[ed] to establish that any such impermissible applications [were] substantial in comparison to the statute's plainly legitimate sweep over unprotected speech and conduct."[166]

In regard to the Fifth and Fourteenth Amendment violations, Bradshaw argued that Texas's statute was unconstitutionally vague because it used an "all encompassing 'harm' standard that would cause potential speakers to steer much further away from the 'unlawful zone of conduct' than would a more narrow statute aimed squarely at unprotected speech."[167] The court rejected this argument as well, concluding that the definition of "harm" provided in relevant penal codes would "sufficiently provide a person of ordinary intelligence fair notice of what the statute prohibits . . . ."[168]

Ex Parte Bradshaw illustrates that carefully crafted anti-catfishing statutes can survive constitutional challenges.[169] The federal anti-catfishing statute proposed in this Article serves the same significant governmental and First Amendment interests in protecting citizens from threats of online impersonation and false speech, as did the Texas statute in *Ex Parte Bradshaw*. Furthermore, the proposed federal statute is more limited than the challenged Texas statute, because it explicitly allows for the satire and parody that Bradshaw argued the Texas statute unconstitutionally precluded.[170]

The proposed statute will also avoid vagueness challenges, as did the statute in *Ex Parte Bradshaw*. The proposed statute clearly defines the term "benefit," for instance, and as seen in *Ex Parte Bradshaw*, the term

---

[165] *Id.* at 677.

[166] *Id.*

[167] *Id.*

[168] *Id.* at 678.

[169] *See generally id.*

[170] *Id.* at 675–76.

"harm" was not unconstitutionally vague when included in an anti-catfishing statute.[171] Given the court's findings in *Ex Parte Bradshaw*, the federal anti-catfishing statute proposed in this Article will likely survive facial challenges to its constitutionality.[172]

ii. Potential Disadvantages to the Proposed Statute

Although a federal anti-catfishing statute is the most effective way to deter and punish catfish predators, and provide redress to catfishing victims, with any solution comes both advantages and disadvantages. One potential downside to a federal anti-catfishing statute is the risk of non-enforcement. Congress enacting a statute does not guarantee that prosecutors will actually use the statute to go after those violating it.[173] However, presence alone of a federal criminal anti-catfishing statute may be enough to deter catfish predators. Even those catfish predators not deterred by a current state statute in their jurisdiction may be deterred by a federal statute because of a greater fear of federal prosecution than state prosecution. Also, because the proposed statute allows for civil claims in addition to criminal charges, claims from catfishing victims may also indirectly help enforce the statute.

Another issue related to a federal anti-catfishing statute is ensuring removal of content after it is deemed harmful in court. Clearly the mere conviction of a catfish predator does not magically remove the harmful content from social media. However, social media websites have policies in place that allow users to request harmful content to be removed.[174]

---

[171] *Id.* at 678.

[172] *Cf.* Young v. American Mini Theatres, Inc., 427 U.S. 50, 61 (1976) (establishing the doctrine that First Amendment attacks on a statute's vagueness or overbreadth will be unsuccessful in federal courts if the statute is "readily subject to a narrowing construction by the state courts.").

[173] *See generally* Robert Heller, Comment, *Selective Prosecution and the Federalization of Criminal Law: The Need for Meaningful Judicial Review of Prosecutorial Discretion*, 145 U. PA. L. REV. 1309, 1314 (1997) (commenting on the "unchecked discretion" of federal prosecutors with charging decisions).

[174] Kori Clanton, Note, *We Are Not Who We Pretend To Be: ODR Alternatives To Online Impersonation Statutes*, 16 CARDOZO J. CONFLICT RESOL. 323, 328 (2014).

Federal injunctions will only make determinations of whether to remove content reported as harmful easier for these websites.[175]

As with any solution, a federal anti-catfishing statute comes with potential downside. Still, the statute proposed in this Article is the most effective way to deter and punish catfish predators, while also providing redress to catfishing victims.

VI. CONCLUSION

Catfishing is a pervasive problem that has the potential to cause severe financial, social, and emotional harms to its victims. Yet the law has not adequately addressed the harms it causes.

The current legal framework surrounding catfishing is comprised of piecemeal laws and claims that ineffectively deter and punish catfish predators. Furthermore, victims of catfishing are often without adequate redress. While a few states have enacted statutes specifically aimed at addressing catfishing, most states still lack legislation addressing the phenomenon. The few state statutes that have been adopted are ineffective due to the lack of uniformity across states, as well as potential jurisdictional challenges that come with the interstate use of the internet in catfishing schemes.

A carefully crafted federal statute designed specifically to address catfishing will best deter and punish catfish predators and provide redress to catfishing victims. This Article thus provides a model federal statute designed to hold catfish predators criminally and civilly liable. The proposed federal statute provides a uniform way to deal with catfishing free from jurisdictional challenges faced by state statutes. Thus, this Article argues that Congress should adopt the proposed statute as a means to address the catfishing phenomenon.

---

[175] *Id.*

DRONES IN CONSTRUCTION

Caroline Loveless[*]

Use of drone technology has rapidly increased in the last few decades. Enhanced capabilities and newfound affordability have allowed drone use to evolve. Drone use is rapidly influencing industries--from agriculture to energy, and environmental to entertainment. Much of the promise of drone technology lies in its potential for use in the construction industry; however, regulations found in 14 C.F.R. § 107 must be relaxed before drones can provide true efficiency in the construction industry and significantly impact the economy.

Similar to regulations of other emerging technologies, federal and state drone regulations are restrictive, reflecting a limited understanding of the technology. Drones enable construction companies to increase productivity, efficiency, worker safety, and OSHA compliance by gathering images, collecting data, reconstructing work schedules, and identifying construction defects. While drones provide inherent benefit to the construction industry, inexperienced operators, faulty mechanics, and limited insurance policies combine to create some risk. However, this risk does not outweigh the benefit that drones provide, and current regulation can be more effectively balanced to reflect the broad benefits of drone operation within the construction industry.

[*] J.D. Candidate 2019, University of Mississippi School of Law.

TABLE OF CONTENTS

I. Introduction

Drones provide many versatile uses that would be of benefit to the construction industry. Drones may be employed at various stages of construction, from land surveying to project completion. Drones provide quick, efficient, and safe acquisition of evidence and data that could help solve many issues plaguing the construction industry. As a generalization, the construction industry strives to complete projects in the quickest amount of time, with the most skill, in the safest manner, and at the lowest cost. Drones can be an effective tool in completing these goals.

Construction is a dangerous business, with hundreds of deaths resulting each year. Companies, managers, and employees constantly strive to promote workplace safety. Safety regulations provide mandates that companies must follow, and penalties are severe if these regulations are violated. Due to their maneuverability and high-quality cameras, drones have incredible monitoring capabilities that can easily identify habitual safety offenders on a construction site. A satisfactory work schedule is critical on a construction site, but delays are inevitable. Drones could document progress and provide relevant parties with pertinent information about the construction site as often as necessary.

Perhaps drones' most attractive qualities are their affordability and their ability to reduce risk in documenting construction sites. While a helicopter or small airplane could be used to gather aerial shots of a construction site, these methods are extremely expensive and costly over time. Additionally, helicopters and small airplanes can be dangerous in downtown areas. These aircraft are too large to navigate in small, confined areas. On the other hand, drones are maneuverable in small spaces and provide the ability for operators to gather extremely detailed information.

Drones are proving to be great assets to many construction sites. Imagine that a large, state-of-the-art hospital is being built in a populous downtown area. The project requires demolition of an old building and construction of the new building. A general contractor, who employs many different subcontractors, is leading the construction of the hospital. As soon as the concrete is poured for the building, heavy rain hits the area for a week. Site inspections cannot be performed because the ground is too muddy for an employer to walk. A drone could be employed to circle the construction site, collecting information to deliver to the general manager and owner.

Imagine you are in a college town, where large apartment complexes are constantly being built. The owner of a substantial commercial real estate group has started building a new property. Because leases have already been signed and housing promised, it is of utmost importance that the project be completed before the fall semester begins. A drone could conduct weekly, or even daily, site inspections to monitor progress and make necessary adjustments to the work schedule.

Picture the installation of new HVAC equipment in a congested downtown area. To install the piece of equipment, a well-developed plan is necessary to reduce risk of delay and injury. A drone could survey the area pre-installation and provide an aerial overview, which could be used to formulate a plan for installation that minimizes the risk of injury to people and properties.

While they possess all these great features, drones are still an emerging technology and therefore come with a small amount of uncertainty. However, these uncertainties, such as potential equipment malfunctions, risk of human injury, or lack of structured drone insurance policies, do not outweigh the substantial benefits that drones provide to the construction industry. As drone technology develops, these weaknesses will become stronger, and the risk of injury and malfunction will be reduced. For example, crash detection and radius sensor technology are quickly becoming standard features on drones.

Currently, the full potential impact of drones on the commercial construction industry is limited by strict regulation and overbroad protections outlined in 14 C.F.R. § 107, which is the Code of Federal Regulations regarding Small Unmanned Aircraft Systems. Drone technology is not so inherently dangerous as to require the amount of protective regulations in place. While the current rules still control, the current administration has signaled a push for deregulation in the drone industry through various statements and proposals. Less strict requirements may be on the horizon.

This paper serves to highlight the ways in which drones will benefit the commercial construction industry. Section II outlines a brief history of the drone and details the relevant differences in drone terminology. Section III depicts the impact of drone technology in other commercial industries, providing insight into the possible applications of these devices in the construction industry. These use-cases also provide a safety and business model for the construction industry to follow. Section IV further describes the unique advantages of drone technology to the construction industry and includes predictions for future construction-drone use. Section V outlines considerations construction companies should review before implementing the technology. Section VI provides an argument for the relaxation of 14 C.F.R. 107, which would enable drones to monitor construction sites efficiently and safely. Finally, Section VII presents a brief conclusion.

II. A BRIEF HISTORY OF SMALL UNMANNED AIRCRAFT

Drones are far from a new phenomenon and were initially introduced as a "vital predecessor" to manned aircraft.[1] Commonly known as "drones," these unmanned aircraft have been in use for centuries—even before the Wright Brothers took their first flight. One of the first recorded instances of the unmanned aircraft was in 425 B.C., when Greek philosopher Archytas used a self-propelling flying device, Flying Pigeon, to understand how birds fly.[2] Although there is much debate about the first actual use of unmanned aircraft, there is a consensus in scholars recognizing their use in battle during the Spanish American War, WWI, the Cold War, and the War on Terror.[3] Drone uses have ranged from aerial

---

[1] DONNA A. DULO, UNMANNED AIRCRAFT IN THE NATIONAL AIRSPACE: CRITICAL ISSUES, TECHNOLOGY, AND THE LAW 9 (2015) [hereinafter DULO].

[2] BENJAMYN I. SCOTT, THE LAW OF UNMANNED AIRCRAFT SYSTEMS: AN INTRODUCTION TO THE CURRENT AND FUTURE REGULATION UNDER NATIONAL, REGIONAL AND INTERNATIONAL LAW 3 (2016) [hereinafter SCOTT] (citing KONSTANTINOS DALAMAGKIDIS ET AL., ON INTEGRATING UNMANNED AIRCRAFT SYSTEMS INTO THE NATIONAL AIRSPACE SYSTEM 12 (Springer 2d ed., 2012)).

[3] *Id.* (citing *History of U.S. Drones*, UNDERSTANDING EMPIRE, https://understandingempire.wordpress.com/2-0-a-brief-history-of-u-s-drones/ (last visited Apr. 1, 2015)); R. Cargill Hall, *Reconnaissance Drones: Their First Use in the Cold War*, 61 AIR POWER HIST. 20 (2014)).

surveillance in the Spanish-American War, jet-propelled surveillance drones during the Cold War, and remote-piloted target strike drones in the War on Terror.[4]

As advances in technology enabled drones to perform a wide variety of functions, a diverse lexicon of terms emerged. Today, there is not consistent agreement on what terms should be used to describe the device. Commonly-used terms include: unmanned aircraft, unmanned aerial vehicle, remote-piloted aircraft, remote-piloted aircraft system, and the catch-all term, drone.[5] The U.S. has referenced commercial drones in its regulations as "unmanned aircraft system[s]" (UAS).[6] It is likely policymakers' choice to refer to the drone as an unmanned aircraft system is related to negative connotations surrounding the use of military drones.[7]

Terminology used is dependent on the drone type and function. Different legal frameworks apply to different drone types and uses. The Federal Aviation Administration (FAA) regulates three primary categories of use: (1) hobbyist and recreational use, (2) governmental and public use, and (3) commercial or civil use.[8] Drones are then further categorized depending on the mechanism of control (unmanned vs. manned) and weight of the machine.[9] For the purposes of this paper, the term "drone" references a commercial-use, unmanned aerial system weighing less than fifty-five pounds.[10]

---

[4] *Id.*

[5] SARAH NILSSON, DRONES ACROSS AMERICA 1 (2017).

[6] SCOTT, *supra* note 2, at 9.

[7] SCOTT, *supra* note 2, at 9.

[8] NILSSON, *supra* note 5 (citing *UAS FAQs*, FEDERAL AVIATION ADMINISTRATION, https://www.faa.gov/uas/faqs (last visited Nov. 22, 2018).

[9] NILSSON, *supra* note 5.

[10] *See UAS FAQs*, FEDERAL AVIATION ADMIN., https://www.faa.gov/uas/faqs (last visited Nov. 22,2018) (requiring registration with the FAA for UAS under fifty-five pounds and

II. Current Applications of Drones in Commercial Industries

While drone technology has existed for centuries, its appeal to commercial industries and hobbyists is largely due to the affordability and range of drone capabilities. In *Drones: Reporting for Work*, Goldman Sachs predicted that the total global spending on drones in the commercial markets would be approximately $100 billion over the next five years.[11] Driving this surge, developments in drone technology have given commercial entities opportunities to collect data in a cost-effective, efficient and safe manner. Commercial drone use is surging both in the U.S. and worldwide.

a. Monitoring Capabilities

One common feature of commercial drones is a high-quality camera, which provides drone owners unprecedented monitoring capabilities. Camera quality ranges with price, but most drones come equipped with a camera capable of producing high-resolution imagery. Drones capture photos and videos at an angle above the subject area, which are stored on a Secure Digital (SD) card, and can be transferred to a computer to analyze and observe.

These photos and videos can be used to monitor aspects of commercial industries that are unique to each sector. For example, data collected from aerial photographs can be used for measuring work quality, detecting problems, solving inefficiencies, monitoring large areas, or even for advertising purposes. The implications stemming from drone videography touch many different commercial industries.

The agricultural industry has already experienced the benefits of drone inspection capabilities. Drones are primarily used to monitor crops

above 0.55 pounds, providing certain operational exemptions to UAS under fifty-five pounds, etc.).

11 *Drones: Reporting for Work*, GOLDMAN SACHS, https://www.goldmansachs.com/insights/technology-driving-innovation/drones, (last visited Nov. 22, 2018) [hereinafter *Drones: Reporting for Work*].

and reduce the manpower needed in crop production.[12] Specifically, farmers and crop managers are using the aerial shots to reduce the inefficiency that comes with multiple farm hands monitoring crops with the "naked eye."[13] The advanced data collection from drones will help detect large areas where crop production has stalled or failed. The visual images that are taken from a couple hundred feet over crops can detect irrigation leaks or identify a waste of resources.[14] Farmers, as well as drone industry specialists, agree that drones "allow for increased production, more efficient management, and lower input costs for chemicals applied to fields."[15] Drones in the agricultural industry can even be used for livestock management by monitoring patterns and habits of the livestock over large areas of land.[16]

The ability of drones to capture high-quality photos and videos has also proven essential to the broadcasting industry, professional sports teams, and the real estate industry. Photos captured can be used to generate income from photography, correct mistakes on the playing field, and

---

[12] *See* Sally French, *This is How Most of the World's Businesses Will Use Drones*, MARKETWATCH (Mar. 18, 2016), http://www.marketwatch.com/story/this-is-how-most-of-the-worlds-businesses-will-use-drones-2016-03-18 (discussing the use of drones "to monitor crop health and identify potentially problematic areas in the field . . . .") [hereinafter French].

[13] Andy Linn, *Agriculture Sector Posted to Soar with Drone Integration, But Federal Regulation May Ground The Industry Before It Can Take Off*, 48 TEX. TECH L. REV. 976, 976 (2016).

[14] Jeff Walsh, *Forget Pizza Delivery: How Drones in Construction and Agriculture Help Save Time and Money*, REDSHIFT BY AUTODESK, (Feb. 18, 2015), https://www.autodesk.com/redshift/drones-in-construction-agriculture-help-save-time-money/.

[15] Emily K. Upchurch, *Drones on the Farm: The Benefits and Controversies Surrounding the Future of Unmanned Aircraft Systems in Agriculture*, 20.2 DRAKE J. OF AGRIC. L. 309, 319 (2016).

[16] *Id.*

advertise properties. NFL teams have used drones to film practices, and FIFA officials have used drones to help referees call plays.[17]

Photos and live-stream video from drones are also used for architectural purposes. Drones are being used in construction of the Sagrada Familia in Barcelona to complete Gaudi's vision and preserve the architectural integrity of the church.[18] As progress on the church is made, the drone captures images and ensures architects that work is being completed properly and in a timely fashion. Photography taken from drones has been used to compile books tracing Moscow's history of architecture.[19]

Another area that could benefit from drone use is wildlife preservation. Drones could be used by park rangers at national parks in Africa to catch rhino poachers.[20] Wildlife biologists have started using drones to follow polar bears in the Arctic, eliminating the need for humans to enter these extreme weather conditions and reducing the helicopters' disturbance of animals.[21] Drones have provided these biologists with more accurate data about the behavior of the polar bears, such as their breeding,

---

[17] Zehra Betul Ayranci, *Use of Drones in Sports Broadcasting*, 33.2 ENT. & SPORTS L. 79, 93 (2017).

[18] Edward Qualtrough, *Sagrada Familia CIO Fernando Villa Interview- Completing Construction on Gaudi's Vision*, CIO INSIGHTS (Mar. 29, 2016), https://www.cio.co.uk/it-strategy/sagrada-familia-cio-interview-3637213/.

[19] Eleanor Gibson, *Denis Esakov uses drone photography to capture Moscow's landmark buildings from above*, DEZEEN (Aug. 24, 2017), https://www.dezeen.com/2017/08/24/spying-on-moscow-a-winged-guide-to-architecture-moscow-architecture-via-drone-denis-esakov-photography/.

[20] Christina Mercer, *How are drone being using? Top companies using drones right now,* TECHWORLD, (Sept. 3, 2018), https://www.techworld.com/picture-gallery/apps-wearables/best-uses-of-drones-in-business-3605145/ [hereinafter Mercer].

[21] Kelly McSweeney, *Wildlife biologists use Intel drones to spy on polar bears*, ZDNET, (Oct. 6, 2017), http://www.zdnet.com/article/wildlife-biologists-use-intel-drones-to-spy-on-polar-bears/.

feeding, and migration patterns.[22] These special devices are also helping indigenous communities around the world to preserve their land, keeping it free from deforestation and encroachment.[23]

b. Use of Drones in Environmental Management and Emergency Response

Taking advantage of the unique benefits of drone technology, the oil and gas industry has begun using drones to manage projects and respond to emergencies. With their ability to quickly gather visual information, drones are becoming a cost-efficient supplement to, or even replacement for, human monitoring. For example, natural gas companies have employed drones to conduct their monthly inspections of equipment. With the ability to fly at speeds up to 40 miles per hour, drones can collect data for over 150 miles in one day.[24] These inspections have previously been conducted using helicopters, which cost up to $2K per hour.[25] At a much cheaper price, drones do not lose any credibility in inspecting equipment either, as they have proven successful in detecting leaks.[26]

Environmentalists have also suggested that drones could be used to detect greenhouse gases and other airborne pollutants.[27] The New York Department of Environmental Conservation began using 22 drones across

---

[22] *Id.*

[23] K.N. Smith, *Indigenous People are Deploying Drones to Preserve Land and Traditions*, DISCOVER MAG. (Dec. 11, 2017, 10:00), http://blogs.discovermagazine.com/crux/2017/12/11/indigenous-drone-land-traditions/#.Wi_79yOZPPA.

[24] *Drones: Reporting for Work*, *supra* note 11.

[25] *Drones: Reporting for Work*, *supra* note 11.

[26] *Drones Simplify Early Detection of Pipeline Leaks,* DRONE DEPLOY (Oct. 17, 2018), https://blog.dronedeploy.com/drones-simplify-early-detection-of-pipeline-leaks-ccf5cc6805bb

[27] Lucas Satterlee, *Climate Drones: A New Tool for Oil and Gas Air Emission Monitoring*, 46 ENVTL. L. INST. 11069 (2016).

the State of New York to "enhance environmental management, conservation, and emergency response efforts."[28] Since the program's inception in September 2017, drones have proven successful in identifying and mapping an oil spill off Staten Island and an eroding coastline on Lake Ontario.[29]

Not only will drones play a role in environmental management, they will also lend a hand for emergency response and crisis management. Richard Patrick, senior advisor of first responder policy for the Department of Homeland Security, while recognizing that more research is needed on drones, commented that drones pose a "definite utility . . . in a broad spectrum of the first responder and homeland security responsibilities."[30] The specific tasks will vary regionally, but drones could be easily sent out to gauge the destruction after a hurricane or predict the path of a raging wildfire.[31] After the devastating Hurricane Irma, 132 drones were deployed for use in the emergency response.[32] Michael Huerta, FAA Administrator, even went as far to say that "hurricane response will be looked back upon as a landmark in the evolution of drone usage in this country."[33] Drones have also been suggested for use in response to landslides and flooding.[34]

---

[28] Betsy Lillian, *New York Dept. of Environmental Conservation Launches 22-Drone Fleet*, UNMANNED AERIAL (Sept. 26, 2017), https://unmanned-aerial.com/new-york-dept-environmental-conservation-launches-22-drone-fleet.

[29] *Id.*

[30] Willie James Inman, *Medical Drones Could Be the Next Wave of Emergency Response*, FOX NEWS (Dec. 14, 2016), http://www.foxnews.com/health/2016/12/14/medical-drones-could-be-next-wave-emergency-response.html.

[31] *Drones: Reporting for Work*, *supra* note 11.

[32] Ken Hanly, *Drone Technology Helping Utility Companies*, DIG. J. (Oct. 21, 2017), http://www.digitaljournal.com/tech-and-science/technology/drone-technology-helping-utility-companies-retain-profitability/article/505669.

[33] *Id.*

[34] DARREN E. PRICE, UNMANNED AIRCRAFT SYSTEMS FOR EMERGENCY MANAGEMENT: A GUIDE FOR POLICY MAKERS AND PRACTITIONERS 9 (2016).

The devices have already been used to fight wildfires, as drones can give a helicopter the best coordinates for a water drop.[35]

c. Delivery System

In December 2016, Amazon Prime began testing a drone delivery system in the United Kingdom and successfully completed a delivery within 13 minutes.[36] The delivery capability of drones has the potential to influence the healthcare industry in many beneficial ways. Medicine and medical supplies could be delivered to rural areas or developing countries. Researchers at Johns Hopkins Hospital are in the process of testing drones to deliver and carry medical specimens like blood and urine samples.[37] The United Nations has employed drones to drop contraceptives over regions in Ghana.[38] Researchers at the William Carey University of Osteopathic Medicine are in the process of developing a drone to carry quick response medical kits to areas affected by natural disasters or terrorist attacks.[39]

d. Commercial Entertainment

Drones have even begun challenging the presence of fireworks in major cities. Many commercial groups and cities around the world are substituting drones for fireworks, pointing to cost efficiency and safety as

---

[35] *Drones: Reporting for Work*, *supra* note 11.

[36] Mercer, *supra* note 20.

[37] Andrea Downing Peck, *Johns Hopkins' Test Drone Travels 161 Miles to Set Record for Delivery Distance of Clinical Laboratory Specimens*, DARK DAILY (Nov. 15, 2017), https://www.darkdaily.com/johns-hopkins-test-drone-travels-161-miles-to-set-record-for-delivery-distance-of-clinical-laboratory-specimens-1115.

[38] Laura Bassett, *Contraception Drones are the Future of Women's Health in Rural Africa*, HUFF. POST (Jan. 27, 2016), https://www.huffingtonpost.com/entry/birth-control-drones-africa_us_56a8a3b4e4b0947efb65fc11.

[39] Ellen Ciurczak, *Carey Doctor, Student Develop Telemedical Drone*, HATTIESBURG AM. (Nov. 8, 2015), http://www.hattiesburgamerican.com/story/news/education/wcu/2015/11/08/carey-doctor-student-develop-telemedical-drone/74336100/.

the two primary reasons.[40] Walt Disney World is incorporating drones in a "Starbright Holiday" celebration, where drones light up the night sky as an alternative to fireworks.[41] Likewise, in Guangzhou, China, almost 1,200 drones recently performed a light show as part of the global economic forum event.[42]

V. APPLICATION TO THE CONSTRUCTION INDUSTRY

In 2016, Goldman Sachs predicted about $11.2 billion will be spent on drones in the construction industry."[43] The report predicted the construction industry would become the highest addressable market for drone job opportunities, followed by the agriculture industry.[44] The most beneficial contribution that drones will make on the construction industry is likely "under the broad heading of project support," which includes investigating, monitoring, and documenting a construction site throughout the course of its development.[45] Drones provide "near-real-time aerial images and software analysis…[and] provide a more comprehensive picture on what's going on," allowing problematic designs or actions to be

---

[40] *See, e.g.*, Liz McLaughlin, *Drones Offer Safe Alternative to Fireworks,* NBC NEWS (July 3, 2018), https://www.wrdw.com/nbc26/content/news/Drones-offer-safer-alternatives-to-fireworks-487235511.html (noting that "[d]rone light shows also alleviate the risk of wildfires, noise and pollution.").

[41] Arthur Levine, *Drones Dazzle at Disney World in a New Holiday Show*, USA TODAY (Dec. 20, 2016), https://www.usatoday.com/story/travel/experience/america/theme-parks/2016/12/20/disney-springs-holiday-drone-show-starbright-holidays/95628500/.

[42] Viola Zhou, *Drones Put on Spectacular Light Show in Southern China*, SOUTH CHINA MORNING POST (Dec. 11, 2017), http://www.scmp.com/news/china/society/article/2123780/drones-put-spectacular-light-show-china.

[43] *Drones: Reporting for Work*, *supra* note 11.

[44] *Drones: Reporting for Work*, *supra* note 11.

[45] Duane Craig, *Using Drones in Construction for Better Project Outcomes*, CONSTR. INFORMER (Nov. 10, 2015), https://constructioninformer.com/using-drones-in-construction-for-better-project-outcomes/.

caught with improved accuracy.[46] With daily drone monitoring, owners and general contractors can identify improper installation or fault work from the moment the mistake occurs. The owner and general contractor may avoid future litigation by identifying problems early in the life of the property.

Drones will also benefit the construction industry by reducing the risk of accidents. Some large-scale construction projects, such as a regional hospital or professional sports stadium, are already using aerial photography as a means of obtaining a progress report.[47] However, in the past, aerial photography required an aircraft or helicopter. The use of drones for some high-risk construction projects, such as a project in a large downtown area, is a safer alternative to using larger aircraft. Wind turbines, which require routine maintenance inspections, serve as another example.[48] Traditionally, these have been accomplished using a three-person team of experienced rope climbers.[49] However, the use of drones can eliminate the health and safety risks to these climbers and decrease the amount of time spent on inspections.[50] The maneuverability, low cost, and quality performance make drones a more desirable option for inspecting cooling towers, bridges, and other structures than would a helicopter or small airplane.[51]

---

[46] Will Knight, *New Boss on Construction Sites is a Drone*, MIT TECH. REV. (Aug. 26, 2015), https://www.technologyreview.com/s/540836/new-boss-on-construction-sites-is-a-drone/.

[47] *Id.*

[48] Adi Gaskell, *Start-up uses drones to maintain wind turbines,* HUFF. POST (Apr. 29, 2016, 4:22 PM), https://www.huffingtonpost.com/adi-gaskell/startup-uses-drones-to-ma_b_9803388.html

[49] *Id.*

[50] *Id.*

[51] *Up and Under – On Using Drones for Bridge Inspection*, WAYPOINT BLOG (Mar. 30, 2016), http://waypoint.sensefly.com/using-drones-uas-for-bridge-inspection/; *UAV Inspection Tools from Microdrones,* MICRODRONES, https://www.microdrones.com/en/industry-experts/inspection/

The following section will enumerate specific areas in which drones will provide clear, real-time documentation of job sites and, in turn, will create more efficient construction practices and reduce ligation.

a. Use of Drones Can Increase Safety Compliance, Reduce Worker Injuries, and Enable Effective Allocation of Liability in Construction Litigation

Regulations play an important role in ensuring safety on a jobsite. Accidents are frequently occurring in the construction industry. In 2015, the construction industry saw 937 fatal injuries.[52] Although accidents are not always preventable, construction companies and workers can use drones to promote worker and site safety. Given the numerous safety regulations imposed on the construction industry, commercial drone use may also improve compliance with these laws -- and will likely do so in a more cost-effective manner.

i. Drones Help Increase Compliance with Occupational Safety and Health Administration (OSHA) Construction Regulations

Construction companies must abide by the minimum standards required by the Occupational Safety and Health Administration (OSHA). OSHA dictates that the prime contractor is responsible for ensuring OSHA compliance.[53] OSHA inspectors enforce regulations and issue fines and penalties for noncompliance.[54] Liabilities stemming from OSHA can be both civil and criminal in nature, with civil penalties ranging from $5,000 to $70,000 per violation.[55] While the prime contractor is responsible, all parties performing work on the construction site must comply with OSHA regulations. Because general contractors are responsible for the jobsite

---

[52] BUREAU OF LABOR STATISTICS, NATIONAL CENSUS OF FATAL OCCUPATIONAL INJURIES IN 2015 (2016).

[53] 29 C.F.R. §§ 1926.16(a), 1926.20 (2018).

[54] WILLIAM ALLENSWORTH ET. AL., CONSTR. LAW 404 (2009).

[55] 29 U.S.C. § 666 (2018).

compliance, they are secondarily liable for any noncompliance of subcontractors or independent contractors.

The ten most frequently cited violations under OSHA are: 1) fall protection, 2) hazard communication, 3) scaffolding, 4) respiratory protection, 5) lockout/tagout, 6) powered industrial trucks, 7) ladders, 8) electrical wiring methods, 9) machine guarding, 10) electrical general requirements.[56] Drones offer a quick and efficient way for contractors to avoid several of these violations. The following are examples of ways in which drones could aid in ensuring OSHA compliance:

A general contractor could use drones to verify subcontractor safety compliance. Drones could easily spot a worker without proper fall protection or a worker without a hardhat and allow the general contractor to reprimand the subcontractor or its workers. By taking a snapshot of the construction site once or twice a day, general contractors can identify workers or subcontracting companies that habitually violate OSHA regulations.

Job foremen are often tasked with performing safety and equipment inspections. While drone use will not entirely relieve the foreman of site inspection duties, the use of the drone will be a significant aid in spotting problems and seeing the job site from a different angle will allow for a more thorough view of the site. Foremen could create more detailed and near-perfect documentation of a safety violation by shooting aerial photographs and capturing the jobsite in real time using a drone. By helping foremen, contractors, and owners identify risks quickly, drones encourage safe, clean, and efficient worksites.

Beyond drone use in prevention, OSHA and other regulatory bodies can utilize this technology post-violation to investigate accidents and determine liability. For example, after an accident on a bridge project in 2017, OSHA fined a contractor $189,000 for improper fall protection and lack of guardrail.[57] In this accident, two employees were severely injured,

---

[56] TOP 10 MOST FREQUENTLY CITED STANDARDS, OSHA (Jan. 5, 2016).

[57] Don McIntosh, *OSHA fines Ross Island Bridge paint contractor $189,000 for safety violations that led to near-fatal accident*, LABORPRESS.ORG (June 20, 2017),

luckily escaping death.[58] Upon receiving notification of the accident, OSHA could have flown a drone around the bridge to assess the project site, gathering data and information that could be helpful in determining penalties. By using a drone to take photos and videos, OSHA would have saved on time and energy required to document all portions of the jobsite.

Aerial jobsite photos are an attractive source of evidence for innocent contractors who have been wrongly accused of contributing to an OSHA violation. If the contractor or subcontractor is wrongfully penalized for a violation, the accused party could defend against OSHA's claims with these photos as evidence of its innocence. These photos, which could act as daily reports, would identify which subcontractor or entity had been working on the area in question prior to the violation.

Although OSHA does not have a specific regulation regarding drone use,[59] OSHA has identified drones as a potential tool in safety regulation and promotion.[60] In the future, OSHA may continue to refrain from addressing the issue of drones, but another, more forward-looking option would be to enact a new provision governing the use of drones on construction sites. If this were to happen, OSHA may categorize the drone as a tool.

ii. Drones Help Avoid Construction Delays

Delays are inevitable in the construction industry. Reasons for construction delays are varied, but some delays are the result of factors

---

https://nwlaborpress.org/2017/06/osha-fines-ross-island-bridge-paint-contractor-189000-for-safety-violations-that-led-to-near-fatal-accident/.

[58] *Id.*

[59] *See* Kevin Druley, *When drones fly*, SAFETY + HEALTH MAG. (May 28, 2017), http://www.safetyandhealthmagazine.com/articles/15626-when-drones-fly ("OSHA Spokesperson Kimberly Darby wrote, 'OSHA does not have a category or specific regulation that governs the use of drones.'").

[60] Fred Hosier, *Could OSHA use drones for safety inspections?*, SAFETY NEWS ALERT (Aug. 3, 2015), http://www.safetynewsalert.com/could-osha-use-drones-for-safety-inspections/

within the control of the general contractor. One common cause for construction delay is having to rework a section of the project because of faulty workmanship. Other causes include: differing site conditions, changes in requirements or design, inclement weather, defective plans and specifications, and owner interference.[61] One of the most critical elements of a construction contract is the work schedule. In fact, most contracts even provide that if a contractor is delayed in finishing the work, the contractor will have to pay liquidated damages for each day past the deadline.[62] One of the most effective ways to stay on track with a construction project's completion schedule is to manage the jobsite and adjust the schedule according to delays.

Drones with aerial photography and video recording capabilities can provide real-time documentation that will allow owners and contractors to adjust a work schedule to accommodate congested work areas. A virtual design team member of Brasfield & Gorrie, a large construction company in the U.S., commented that "[design teams] can plan workflows and develop . . . site logistics plans that identify high-traffic areas, crane clearances, and areas where materials will move in and out."[63] Consider the effect that photos of immense water pileup from a heavy rainstorm could have on an owner. The owner might become more understanding and acknowledge that the work schedule should be adjusted. Furthermore, there is a possibility that owners would interfere less if they have aerial updates of the work progress.[64]

---

[61] *See generally* Barry B. Bramble & Michael T. Callahan, CONSTR. DELAY CLAIMS (6th ed. 2017).

[62] L. FRANKLIN ELMORE, FUNDAMENTALS OF CONSTRUCTION LAW 223 (2013).

[63] Jeff Link, *Here Comes the Next Big Technological Boom: Drones in Construction*, REDSHIFT (Nov. 17, 2016), https://www.autodesk.com/redshift/drones-in-construction/ [hereinafter Link].

[64] Will Knight, *Construction Drones*, 118 MIT TECH. REV. 17.

iii. Drone Imaging Can Provide Useful Evidence in Construction Litigation Matters

Drones can be used in a variety of ways to prevent construction defect claims, which is one of the largest areas of construction litigation. These legal claims arise in many different contexts, but typically involve a negligent party. For example, a contractor may fail to follow plans and specifications and incur liability.[65]

Drones with thermal energy technology could show the presence of technical constructive anomalies, which would put builders on alert.[66] Drones would be extremely beneficial when there is a heavy downpour to show which areas of the site are still passable. Videography from drones could monitor erosion silt fences, which are used to block mud washing away from the jobsite after a heavy downpour, to make sure they are still functioning and in place.

Catching construction defects early is important.[67] Defects can harm the environment, lead to bad business practices, create cash-flow issues, cause accidents, delay projects, and, of course, cost more money.[68] Most states have a strict statute of limitations that restricts the amount of time in which a lawsuit alleging defective claims can be brought.[69] With

---

[65] Steven B. Lesser & Ryan F. Carpenter, *My Favorite Mistakes: An Owner's Guide to Avoiding Disaster on Construction Projects*, 37 SPG CONST. LAW. 6, 13 (Spring 2017); Kate Murphy, *Shifting Soil Threatens Homes' Foundations*, THE N.Y. TIMES (Mar. 3, 2010), http://www.nytimes.com/2010/03/04/garden/04foundation.html.

[66] Raluca Pleşu, Gabriel Teodoriu & George Ţăranu, *Infrared Thermography Applications for Building Investigation,* "Gheorghe Asachi" Technical University of Iaşi (Mar. 20, 2012), http://www.bipcons.ce.tuiasi.ro/Archive/287.pdf.

[67] *See generally* Paul Netscher, *The true costs of poor quality construction*, ACCEDE (Jan. 22, 2017), http://accedeglobal.com/actual-cost-of-poor-quality-on-construction-project/.

[68] *See generally id.* (discussing the many problems resulting from construction defects).

[69] *E.g.*, Carl E. Woodward, L.L.C. v. Acceptance Indem. Ins. Co., 743 F.3d 91, 101 (5th Cir. 2014) (discussing Mississippi's statute of limitations as it applies to construction defects).

the help of constant monitoring by drones, these problems can be caught during operations, instead of after completion of the project. Settlements of construction defect claims can be extremely costly. For example, improper installation of window and door flashing on a 300-unit housing complex in Newport, California led to a settlement of over eight figures.[70] While the project was completed in 2006, the construction defects were not recognized until 2015.

Detailed and full documentation of a construction project is essential to successfully defending or asserting construction claims. Often, construction concepts are complex and unique. This presents a hurdle for lawyers who must explain the issue at hand to jurors or judges unfamiliar with construction terminology. Similarly, photos taken on mid-sized construction sites are often taken by a camera without a wide-angle lens, making it difficult to discern specific issues the photos depict and where the snapshots were taken.[71] A high-quality drone camera would eliminate the issue of shoddy photography, and the wide-angle shots from the drone would put the issue into perspective.[72] Aerial photographs will soon become essential in construction litigation because they "can clarify or explain oral testimony or documentary narrative in concrete terms."[73]

b. Drones Provide More Effective Mapping Pre-Construction

As the technology continues to develop, drones will be essential to land surveying. A recent survey found that 52% of the respondents in the

---

[70] Trey Barrineau, *Major Construction-Defect Lawsuit Settled*, DOOR & WINDOW MARKET MAG, (Dec. 1, 2016), https://www.dwmmag.com/major-construction-defect-lawsuit-settled/.

[71] Morgan Smith, *Building the Visual Foundation of Your Construction Defect Case*, COGENT LEGAL (Nov. 5, 2013), http://cogentlegal.com/blog/2013/11/visual-construction-defect-case/.

[72] Christopher G. Hill, *The 6 Essentials of Construction Photography*, CONSTR. L. MUSINGS (Oct. 14, 2015), http://constructionlawva.com/6-essentials-construction-photography/.

[73] *See* THOMAS J. KELLEHER, JR. ET. AL., COMMON SENSE CONSTRUCTION LAW 508 (2005).

construction industry have considered using drones for land surveying, thermal imaging, or scanning.[74] The primary attraction for companies using drones to survey land is the reduction of time spent in the early stages of construction.[75]

Traditional land surveys could take weeks, but a drone can complete a land survey in a matter of hours.[76] Mapping with a drone will speed up specific stages of production time. One commenter notes that "in a recent exercise to verify site work for a 61-acre Florida Hospital Apopka project, [he] estimates that surveying a site with a drone helped provide nearly a 75 percent time savings."[77] Likewise, another construction company used drones to produce 3D maps of terrain and cut the time spent surveying a property by 98%.[78]

In addition to surveying, drones are also used to find the proposed grade on a construction site. This has been done by measuring distance through a cloud of data points and converting the information into an elevation map and a 3D model.[79] Ultimately, enabling land surveyors and construction operators to get a full picture of the property before construction begins will allow for more effective and efficient job completion. Therefore, the use of drones in the construction industry will

---

[74] Godfrey Hoffman, *The Use of Drone Technology for Land Surveying of Constr. Projects* (Sept. 22, 2017), http://www.godfreyhoffman.com/blog/the-use-of-drone-technology-for-land-surveying-of-construction-projects.

[75] *Id.*

[76] *Land Surveys,* MILE HIGH DRONES, http://www.milehighdrones.com/land-surveys.html (last visited Nov. 22, 2018).

[77] Link, *supra* note 63.

[78] French, *supra* note 12.

[79] Link, *supra* note 63.

improve the entire lifecycle of the industry, from pre-build to post-completion.[80]

V. POTENTIAL DRONE LIABILITIES TO CONSIDER

Although drones will provide substantial benefits to the construction industry, these benefits do not come without a cost. If improperly operated, drones have the potential to injure construction workers or damage expensive machinery on the job site. Like any new technology, drones can be subject to malfunction. However, there are a substantial number of ways for this risk to be calculated and allocated. While these risks are inherent in the use of drones, they do not outweigh the benefits of drone use in the construction world.

a. Injury to Person or Property

One of the most critical concerns for drone use on the construction site is the potential for injury to a construction worker or damage to expensive equipment or finished work. This concern alone may be the reason for the strict guidelines and regulations governing commercial drone use.

The following examples present real-world situations where a drone could produce an exponential number of liabilities on a construction site. Imagine a general contractor flying a drone over a large construction site, gathering images to show to the property owner. The drone malfunctions and suddenly strikes a subcontractor's construction worker, propelling him off his elevated position on scaffolding. The man is seriously injured as a result of the drone striking him, and his injuries are potentially fatal. In this scenario, it is uncertain whether liability falls to the owner, general contractor, operator, or employer. Imagine a similar situation where a drone operator loses control or sight of his drone, and the drone subsequently crashes into a large glass window or someone making deliveries to the construction site.

---

[80] *See* Link, *supra* note 63 (noting ways in which drones will improve the construction industry).

As drones are being used more frequently in commercialized settings, accidents are becoming more prevalent.[81] A couple of high-profile incidents have recently occurred. Although no one was injured, the crowd at an MLB game was quickly placed on guard when a drone flew into the stands.[82] In another incident, a cyclist flipped over his handlebars in a bike race after a drone crashed into his front wheel.[83]

Not only will the owner or operator of the drone possibly face personal liability to the injured, he or she will also have a duty to report the accident to the FAA.[84] A severe accident could potentially lead to the revocation of a license to operate.[85] Likewise, the FAA and New Jersey both have penalties of their own for flying under the influence of alcohol.[86]

b. Products Liability

Like any new technology, drone manufacturers will likely incur products liability claims in the future. Product liability claims can arise

---

[81] *See* Conner Forrest, *17 drone disasters that show why the FAA hates drones*, TECHREPUBLIC (Jun. 13, 2018), https://www.techrepublic.com/article/12-drone-disasters-that-show-why-the-faa-hates-drones/.

[82] Fitz Tepper, *The FAA gets a case study with a drone crash inside an MLB stadium*, TECHCRUNCH (May 2017), https://techcrunch.com/2017/05/23/the-faa-gets-a-case-study-with-a-drone-crash-inside-an-mlb-stadium/.

[83] Craig Cunningham, *Drone crashes into cyclist mid-race*, CYCLING WEEKLY (May 2017), http://www.cyclingweekly.com/videos/watch/watch-drone-crashes-cyclist-mid-race.

[84] 14 C.F.R. § 107.9.

[85] *See* FEDERAL AVIATION ADMINISTRATION, LAW ENFORCEMENT GUIDANCE FOR SUSPECTED UNAUTHORIZED UAS OPERATIONS (Aug. 14, 2018), https://www.faa.gov/uas/resources/law_enforcement/media/FAA_UAS-PO_LEA_Guidance.pdf.

[86] *See* 14 CFR § 107.57; Josh Russell, *New Jersey Gets Tough on Drunken Drone Pilots*, COURTHOUSE NEWS (Dec. 8, 2017, 12:07 PM), https://www.courthousenews.com/new-jersey-gets-tough-on-drunken-drone-pilots/.

through economic losses and human injury.[87] "A drone is a tool, much like a dozer or a crane, and like those vital pieces of equipment, it must be continually evaluated for operational and job safety."[88] One way for drone owners to limit potential future liability is through proactive planning and risk management. Drone manufacturers follow standard risk-management processes. Two examples of management processes include ISO 31000 Risk Management–Guidelines and the International Electrotechnical Commission's IEC 61508 on functional safety of electrical, electronic, and programmable safety-related systems.[89] These processes are industry standards that certify high quality, well-made drones.[90] Drone owners should consider whether their drones follow these guidelines and evaluate the pros and cons for each system.[91] By doing so, commercial companies can ensure that drones meet industry standards, thereby eliminating the risk of ill-equipped drones.

However, not all drone manufacturers will follow common industry standards or best practices. Owners and operators of drones should be aware of the potential for product malfunction. For construction parties interested in purchasing a drone and training management to operate it, best practices and industry standards for drone manufacturing should be evaluated. By proactively determining the best practices and industry standards, construction companies may choose a drone with less potential to injure a construction employee or cause property damage.

c. Risk Allocation and Mitigation

Construction companies that plan on purchasing a drone should consider ways to allocate their risk. A general contractor could allocate the

---

[87] DULO, *supra* note 1, at 258.

[88] Aldo Fucentese & Mike Mills, *Managing the Insurance Implications of Construction Drones*, INS. TODAY III (Nov. 2016).

[89] DULO, *supra* note 1, at 276.

[90] DULO, *supra* note 1, at 276.

[91] DULO, *supra* note 1, at 274.

risks to subcontractors through indemnification and insurance provisions in a contract.

Another way for construction companies to mitigate liability when using drones is to contract with a third-party drone firm that has its own insurance. Drone firms are rapidly popping up throughout the country and are becoming essential to many large construction companies.[92] In this way, instead of conducting the drone surveillance in-house, a construction company would hire a third-party to operate the drone and provide the data required for the construction project. As such, the typical construction insurance schema would not be interrupted. The drone company, acting as the subcontractor, could list the general contractor as an additional insured on its insurance policy if the contract so provides.

Construction companies could also rent drones and maintain insurance on the drone through a rental company, like they do with other equipment rentals. Although costlier, the construction company would be able to avoid the inherent risks that come with drone ownership. Most construction equipment is rented and insured through the rental company. This schema could provide guidance for drone use.

d. Insurance

The current drone regulations do not require an insurance policy for commercial drone use. This is not unique for the FAA, as manned aircraft are not mandated to have insurance either.[93] While there is no requirement for manned aircraft to be insured, it would be foolish for aircraft companies to neglect to insure their aircraft. In the same sense, construction entities should obtain insurance before placing drones into flight. The risk of monetary liability that comes with the risk for injury to person and property is entirely too substantial for construction entities to not have insurance on the device.

---

[92] *E.g.*, DRONE AMERICA, www.droneamerica.com; DRONEZONE, https://www.dronezon.com/; DUTCH DRONE COMPANY, www.dutchdronecompany.com.

[93] SCOTT, *supra* note 2, at 90.

Many supporters of drone integration into the commercial industry have advocated for required drone liability insurance. Industry consultants have gone so far as to say that "insurability is a necessary event before businesses can successfully use UAS in the National Airspace System." [94] Specific arguments for mandatory insurance include: (1) other countries require drone insurance, (2) liability insurance encourages safe operation of drone equipment, and (3) drone operations are analogous to automobile operations, which require liability insurance.[95] In response, the FAA has declared that it does not possess the authority to mandate insurance for drone operators.[96]

Insurance coverage for drone owners and operators is still in its infancy.[97] However, insurance is an adaptive industry, meaning that companies will begin to develop more drone-specific policies in the context of liability insurance as drone use increases. For example, cranes, excavators, and forklifts create a substantial risk on the construction site that requires insurance, much like drones would. The cost of securing adequate insurance coverage may preclude some mid-market and small construction companies from using drones, which may in turn incentivize the use of drone firms mentioned above.

Whether the construction company chooses to operate drones in-house or by hiring a drone firm, they should not operate without some form of insurance. While insurance companies currently have an offering of

---

[94] SCOTT, *supra* note 2, at 288 (quoting Brianna Ehley, *What's Grounding the Commercial Drone Industry?*, THE FIN. TIMES (May 21, 2013), http://www.thefiscaltimes.com/Articles/2013/05/21/Whats-Grounding-the-Commercial-Drone-Industry).

[95] TIMOTHY M. RAVICH, COMMERCIAL DRONE LAW: DIGEST OF U.S. AND GLOBAL UAS RULES, POLICIES, AND PRACTICES 222 (2017).

[96] *Id.*; Operation and Certification of Small Unmanned Aircraft Systems, 81 Fed. Reg. 42,064, 42,183 (Jun. 28, 2016) (codified as 14 C.F.R. pt. 107).

[97] SCOTT, *supra* note 2, at 90.

drone coverage, as time progresses and drones continue to enter commercial markets, insurance policies will become more drone friendly.[98]

'I. Legal Restrictions Preventing Drones from Reaching their Full Potential

a. Need for Deregulation of Drones

Recognizing the need for incorporating drones into the national airspace, the FAA has worked towards integration since 2008.[99] Prior to 2016, individuals and companies seeking to use drones for commercial purposes had to apply for an exception under the Section 333 provision of the FAA Modernization and Reform Act of 2012.[100] In June 2016, the FAA released final rules for civil small unmanned aircraft systems within the U.S.[101] The rules took effect on August 29, 2016.[102] The new rules substantially relax the FAA's previous rules on commercial drone use.[103] In its notice of proposed rulemaking, the FAA claimed that the restrictions placed on operation were "in order to maintain the safety of the [National Airspace System] and ensure that [small unmanned aircraft systems] do not pose a threat to national security."[104] Section 107 includes regulations

---

[98] KELLEHER, *supra* note 73; Paul J. Bauer, *Emerging Use of Drones Raises Insurance Issues*, 38 N.H. BUS. REV. 36 (Feb. 19, 2016).

[99] *See* FEDERAL AVIATION ADMINISTRATION, PART 107 OF THE FEDERAL AVIATION REGULATIONS, https://www.faa.gov/uas/media/RIN_2120-AJ60_Clean_Signed.pdf.

[100] Bill Carey, FAA Issues 76 Waivers as Part 107 Drone Rule Takes Effect, AIN ONLINE (Aug. 29, 2016, 3:50 PM), https://www.ainonline.com/aviation-news/business-aviation/2016-08-29/faa-issues-76-waivers-part-107-drone-rule-takes-effect.

[101] 14 C.F.R. § 107 (2016).

[102] *Id.*

[103] *See* Andy Pasztor, *U.N. Aviation Arm Seeks to Establish Global Drone Guidelines*, WALL STREET J. (Sept. 21, 2017), https://www.wsj.com/articles/u-n-aviation-arm-seeks-to-establish-global-drone-guidelines-1505986201?mg=prod/accounts-wsj ("[i]n the U.S. . . . commercial drones were basically banned from the skies until 2016.").

[104] Notice of Proposed Rulemaking Part 107, 80 Fed. Reg. 9543, 9546 (Feb. 23, 2015).

governing registration, airman certification, and operation of civil small unmanned aircraft systems within the U.S.[105] While 14 C.F.R. § 107 allows commercial drone operation, the regulations are too strict and far from ideal. The rapid development of drones as a new technology has sparked government attention across the world. A balance must be struck between ensuring safety and health and utilizing the powerful benefits of drones. Obtaining this balance has proven tricky for policymakers and regulators worldwide.

Technology and regulation are constantly in conflict. Many scholars have commented that technology represents growth and progress, while regulation represents bureaucracy and government.[106] However, scholars also agree that "[t]he influence of regulation on technology is critically dependent on the technology of regulation."[107] Eli Dourado, director of the Technology Policy Program at George Mason University, noted that "at a micro level…individual regulations are holding back future technology."[108]

Advocates for allowing new technology to immediately enter interstate commerce have coined the term "permissionless innovation," which encourages free experimentation without public official blessing. Basically, the permission to experiment with new technology should be "permitted by default."[109] Permissionless innovation means that "unless a compelling case can be made that a new invention will bring serious harm to society, innovation should be allowed to continue unabated and

---

[105] 14 C.F.R. § 107.

[106] *See* Jonathan B. Wiener, *The regulation of technology, and the technology of regulation*, 26 TECH. IN SOCIETY 483, 484 (2004).

[107] *Id.*

[108] James Pethokoukis, *Is regulation slowing tech progress and innovation? A Q&A with Eli Dourado*, AEI IDEAS (June 3, 2016), http://www.aei.org/publication/big-government-regulation-slowing-tech-progress-eli-dourado/.

[109] Adam Thierer, *Embracing a Culture of Permissionless Innovation*, CATO INST. ONLINE FORUM, (Nov. 17, 2014), https://www.cato.org/publications/cato-online-forum/embracing-culture-permissionless-innovation.

problems, if they develop at all, can be addressed later."[110] This idea is in direct competition with the "precautionary principle," which refers to the idea that innovations should wait to be released until the manufacturers can illustrate to policy makers that no harm will be caused to the public.[111]

Permissionless innovation supporters argue that innovation with a precautionary mindset results in a decline in the overall standard of living through less services, inferior goods at increased prices, and diminished economic growth.[112] Specifically applied to drones, permissionless innovation will do no harm, because commercial drones are not inherently dangerous.[113] One researcher predicted that "a drone is likely to collide with other aircraft about once every 374,000 years of continuous operation."[114] With such low likelihood of a catastrophic accident, the tight regulations surrounding commercial drones should be relaxed to allow for economic growth and efficiency in business.

b. Why Relaxation of 14 C.F.R. § 107 is Necessary and How to Do It

The current commercial drone regulation, 14 C.F.R. § 107, severely limits the positive impact drones could have on the construction industry. For example, 14 C.F.R. § 107 requires that the visual observer and the drone operator must view the unmanned aircraft throughout the entirety of the flight.[115] Although the current regulation provides a list of waivable

---

[110] *Id.* at 3.

[111] *Id.*

[112] *Id.*

[113] *See* Eli Dourado, *Creating an Environment of Permissionless Innovation for Unmanned Aircraft*, MERCATUS CTR. (Mar. 10, 2016), https://www.mercatus.org/publication/creating-environment-permissionless-innovation-unmanned-aircraft ("[T]he best evidence shows that commercial drones do not pose a serious risk to the airspace.").

[114] *Id.*

[115] 14 C.F.R. § 107.31 (2016).

requirements for the drone operator, the option for waiver has the effect of allowing the FAA to consider the applicability of regulations on an ad hoc basis.[116] As commercial drone use continues to expand, constantly addressing waiver will become an administrative burden on the FAA and a high-cost activity for construction companies. While most of these provisions will likely be subject to less regulation in the future due to the waiver option,[117] I argue that there are three specific elements of the current regulation that should be adapted to reflect the extensive benefits that drones will have on the construction industry. Specifically, the law should be adapted to allow for: (1) the drone to fly outside of the visual sight of the operator, (2) the ability to fly drones over people, and (3) expanding the allowed distance between a drone and operator beyond three miles.

i. Drones Should Be Allowed to Fly Beyond Line of Sight

For drones to fully serve commercial industries, regulations must allow flight operation beyond the line of sight. This would enable agricultural parties to fly drones for miles over crops, inspecting for irrigation or growth problems. Likewise, oil and gas industries would benefit from the increased ability to fly long-distances. On large construction sites it may not be practical for the drone to stay in the line of sight of the operator. If a drone is inspecting a tower or bridge, the drone may need to get into a tight space that is blocked from view. The line of sight restriction prevents the drone from acting as a safer inspection mechanism. For example, a drone could be used to conduct bridge inspections instead of a helicopter. However, if the drone is limited to staying within the visual sight line, the drone's full potential is squashed.

---

[116] *See* 14 C.F.R. § 107.205 (listing examples such as operation from a moving vehicle or aircraft, daylight operation, visual line of sight aircraft operation, visual observer, operation of multiple small unmanned aircraft systems, yielding the right of way, operation over people, operation in certain airspace, and operating limitations for small unmanned aircraft.)

[117] 14 C.F.R. § 107.205(c).

ii. Drones Should Be Allowed to Fly Over Humans

Current drone regulations also prohibit drone operation over human beings unless the person is located under a covered structure or inside a stationary vehicle.[118] Effectively, this requirement limits drone use on construction sites to times when employees are not on site. While the FAA is an agency designed to promote safety, the inability to fly over people effectively prevents drone use in the construction industry. In doing so, the regulations hinder the ability for drones to carry out safety and environmental regulation compliance. While FAA's waiver provision may grant a construction company the ability to employ a drone,[119] this step creates inefficiency for the FAA and proves burdensome for commercial industries with a desire to use a drone. Allowing flight over people will benefit other commercial industries as well as construction. Sports journalism and mass media would have the opportunity to capture incredible aerial shots of events with fans present.

iii. The Permissible Distance Between Operator and Drone Should Be Expanded

Currently, drone operators are allowed no less than 3 miles between the physical operator and the drone while in flight.[120] Road construction entities would see significant benefits with the relaxation of this provision. The Oregon Department of Transportation recognizes the benefit that drones would provide in improving the "precision and accuracy of construction projects" and is currently investigating the possibility of using a drone to survey road projects.[121]

---

[118] 14 C.F.R. § 107.39.

[119] 14 C.F.R. § 107.205(d).

[120] 14 C.F.R. § 107.51.

[121] Charles Choi, *Drone Surveys Improve Automated Road Construction*, INSIDE UNMANNED SYS. (Oct. 28, 2016), http://insideunmannedsystems.com/drone-surveys-improve-automated-road-construction/.

While further relaxation to this drone regulation will only provide minimal benefits to the construction industry, increased distance would allow other industries to thrive on drone technology. Specifically, the ability to monitor pipeline without such tight distance limits would significantly benefit the oil and gas industry. Likewise, the agricultural sector would benefit if a farmer could monitor 1,000 acres a day, without having to maintain visual sight on the drone. Environmental groups and city planners could also substantially benefit from flying a drone outside a three-mile radius of the operator. Section 107's limit on distance is the provision that disables companies like Amazon from using drones as delivery vehicles.[122] For this reason, Amazon has chosen to test its drone technology in the United Kingdom.[123] Likewise, this provision also prevents a clinic in Southwest Virginia from delivering medication to rural Americans.[124] In the future, the FAA should eliminate the regulations that require a certificate of waiver.

Currently, there are no standards regarding the manufacturing and production of drones. The FAA's focus should be on developing and mandating uniform standards that require every drone to be equipped with certain safeguards. The use of safeguards will eliminate the need for strict operational regulations. For example, collision avoidance mechanisms could detect objects in the path of the drone and either change the flight

---

[122] Andrew Meola, *Shop Online and Get Your Item Delivery by a Drone Delivery Service*, BUS. INSIDER (Jul. 18, 2017), https://www.businessinsider.com/delivery-drones-market-service-2017-7

[123] Christina Mercer & Margi Murphy, *Best uses of drones: How 24 companies are using drones*, TECHWORLD (Sept. 6, 2017), https://www.techworld.com/picture-gallery/apps-wearables/best-uses-of-drones-in-business-3605145/; Michael Laris, *Trump administration to allow quick and dramatic expansion of drone use*, WASH. POST (Oct. 25, 2017), https://www.washingtonpost.com/local/trafficandcommuting/trump-administration-establishing-innovation-zones-for-widespread-drone-use/2017/10/25/a004b400-b990-11e7-9e58-e6288544af98_story.html?utm_term=.37d98ef42c77.

[124] Teresa Gardner, *Drone-delivered health care in rural Appalachia*, CLINICAL ADVISOR (Dec. 6, 2016), http://www.clinicaladvisor.com/practice-management-information-center/drone-delivered-health-care-in-rural-appalachia/article/576891/.

pattern of the drone to avoid the objects, or cause the drone to brake.[125] Also, increased use of optical flow sensors will allow more drones to operate autonomously.[126]

c. Preemption Issues

Once a new technology has been introduced, competition between state law and federal law typically ensues. Past examples of the complex interaction between state and federal law governing new technology include factories, railroads, television, telephones, the internet, and biotechnology.[127] The confusion surrounding the interplay between federal, state, and local drone law is not a new phenomenon. One argument is that federal law should control drone laws, since drone usage in the aggregate will affect interstate commerce.[128] However, another argument is that state and local law should have precedent over federal law in governing drones because privacy law affects local constituents.[129]

Aviation is primarily governed by federal law, since Congress gave the FAA the authority to regulate airspace use, management and efficiency, air traffic control, safety, navigational facilities, and aircraft noise.[130] The purpose of the FAA holding sole authority on this matter is to maintain a

[125] Jake Wilkinson, *The Future of Drone Technology - Autonomy, Collison Avoidance and Advanced Sensors*, AZO SENSORS (Apr. 25, 2017), https://www.azosensors.com/article.aspx?ArticleID=782.

[126] *Id.*

[127] Henry H. Perritt, Jr., *One Centimeter Over My Backyard: Where Does Federal Preemption of State Drone Regulation Start?*, 17 N.C. J.L. & TECH 307, 310–11 (2015).

[128] *See generally id.* at 326–48 (discussing how aviation interacts with the Commerce Clause and federal preemption).

[129] FED. AVIATION ADMIN., OFFICE OF THE CHIEF COUNSEL, STATE AND LOCAL REGULATION OF UNMANNED AIRCRAFT SYSTEMS (UAS) FACT SHEET, (2015).

[130] *Id.*

safe and sound air transportation system.[131] Part 107 does not include a preemption provision in its framework. Congress has vested with the FAA the power to regulate airspace.[132] However, many states and municipalities have enacted drone legislation. This federal, state, and local web of rules and regulations surrounding drone usage has left drone users and courts uncertain of which laws apply.

Part 107 does not prevent states or municipalities from enacting legislation governing drones. However, there are some provisions in Part 107 that give complete authority to the FAA. First, the FAA's requirement for federal regulation in registration of a drone are the only means for registering.[133] This means no states may advance more strict rules without first obtaining FAA approval. Secondly, the FAA has complete control over regulating the federal airspace. The FAA has produced a Fact Sheet detailing the regulatory framework for use by states and localities when considering laws affecting drones. The Fact Sheet mandates that states and localities should be consistent with the FAA regulations when creating rules and policies for the use of drones. The FAA does not claim field preemption for UAS laws, meaning the FAA allows state and localities to produce certain drone laws. When conflict arises between the state and federal laws, the federal government has noted that preemption will be dealt with in a case-specific analysis.

While the FAA has preemption over a couple specific issues, the agency encourages state and local consultation with the FAA. The use of drones intersects with legal areas typically reserved for the state police power—including land use, zoning, privacy, trespass, and law enforcement operations. Drone issues in these fields are generally subject to state and local regulation.[134] Examples of situations where state and local law would control include the following: requiring police forces to obtain a warrant when using drones as surveillance, prohibiting the use of drones for hunting

---

[131] *Id.*

[132] 49 U.S.C. § 40103 (2018).

[133] NILSSON, *supra* note 5, at 33.

[134] NILSSON, *supra* note 5, at 33.

and fishing, and prohibiting the attachment of a firearm or weapon to a drone.[135] The following are examples promulgated by the FAA where consultation would be encouraged: 1) cities wanting to ban UAS operation within city limits or within certain distances of landmarks; and 2) mandating equipment or training for UAS operation.[136]

In *Singer v. City of Newton*, the first federal court decision concerning drone preemption, the court held that a city ordinance requiring drone registration with the city were preempted by federal laws.[137] In its September 2017 decision, the court held that Part 107 is the sole authority with the ability to require registration. The decision also declared that federal airspace limits are entirely federal. Specifically, the FAA has authority to "prescribe air traffic regulations on the flight of aircraft."[138] Therefore, states and cities may not restrict the altitude of drone flights to anything above federally regulated altitudes.[139]

The effect of this decision by a federal district court judge grants a large amount of deference to the FAA in authority and decision-making. However, it is still unclear whether this authority will remain with the FAA. In October 2017, just one month after the court's decision in *Singer*, President Trump declared a new vision concerning the future of drone law in the United States.[140] Specifically, Trump's memorandum granted the Transportation Secretary the ability to administer a pilot program for drones, which allows state, local and tribal governments to create

---

[135] NILSSON, *supra* note 5, at 33.

[136] NILSSON, *supra* note 5, at 33.

[137] 2017 U.S. Dist. LEXIS 153844, 11–12.

[138] 49 U.S.C. § 40103(b)(2) (2018).

[139] 2017 U.S. Dist. LEXIS 153844, 11–12.

[140] *See generally* Michael Laris, *Trump administration to allow quick and dramatic expansion of drone use*, WASH. POST (Oct. 25, 2017), https://www.washingtonpost.com/local/trafficandcommuting/trump-administration-establishing-innovation-zones-for-widespread-drone-use/2017/10/25/a004b400-b990-11e7-9e58-e6288544af98_story.html?utm_term=.63fbd66bf0d7.

innovation zones.[141] This program will push forward the permissionless innovation many technology policy makers desire, and will open the door to unprecedented economic benefits.

In response to this proposal, Michael Kratsios, Deputy Assistant to the President at the White House Office of Science and Technology Policy, notes that "opening American skies to infrastructure inspections and emergency management operations, and enabling commerce will be broadly beneficial and provide the government with data for rewriting regulations."[142] The FAA is hopeful that the program will help create regulations that balance local and national interests as well as address security and privacy risks.[143] Specifically, the program is designed to speed up the current process for approving waivers for operations that require special permission from the FAA.[144]

VII. CONCLUSION

As drone technology improves, the positive impact on commercial business will continue to expand. As an industry plagued by inefficiencies, the construction sector will substantially benefit from the use of commercial drones. Drones will increase productivity by detecting safety violations, construction defects, and delays in the work schedule. Likewise, drones can speed up specific stages of construction work, like site surveying and regularly scheduled site inspections. Aerial images and videos from drones will keep owners and general contractors informed of the activities and progress on job sites.

Although the construction industry has the potential to exponentially benefit from the use of drones, current regulations are too

---

141 *Id.*

142 *Id.*

143 News Update, Fed. Aviation Admin. (Oct. 25, 2017), https://www.faa.gov/news/updates/?newsId=89007&omniRss=news_updateAoc&cid=101_N_U.

144 *Id.*

strict. These regulations, which require drones to fly inside the sight of the operator, prohibit drones from flying over people, and mandate a maximum distance of three miles between the operator and the drone, hinder the construction industry from experiencing the full impact of drones. The current administration's recent memorandum ordering innovation zones signals a transition from precautionary regulation making towards permission-less innovation in the drone industry. Although the creation of innovation zones will not repeal 14 C.F.R. § 107, or immediately relax the current regulations, the zones signal a move towards less strict regulations.

In the near future, the commercial construction industry can expect to see the decline of regulations concerning the use of drones. Specifically, most waiver provisions in 14 C.F.R. § 107 will likely be repealed as detection sensors emerge as a normal feature of drone technology. If these regulations are relaxed, the construction industry will benefit from increased efficiencies through monitoring, problem identification, crisis response, and delivery.

PRESS A TO PAY: PAYMENT PROCESSING WITHIN VIRTUAL WORLDS

*Hunter Barker**

"The best solution to a problem is usually the easiest one..." - GLaDOS, Portal 2

* J.D., 2017, University of Texas School of Law. Very few cases have directly considered many of the problems addressed in this paper. As a result, most of the analysis is based primarily on future predictions and the various possibilities that developers might want to consider when implementing payment systems in their games. This note attempts to give horizontal advice across the industry for developers faced with this changing landscape of payment processing.

TABLE OF CONTENTS

I. INTRODUCTION

In the early 2000s, Bungie released an add-on for its blockbuster game: Halo 2. This add-on consisted of additional maps the player could download to his Xbox and use online with his friends. To acquire the add-on, a player would likely drive to their local gaming store, pay $29.99 to the cashier, receive the product, drive home, and insert the disc into the Xbox. The player could also share the disc with his friends, allowing all of them to download the add-on as well—reminiscent of early videogame piracy.[1] This type of exchange was preventable by the early 2000s, illustrating several challenges facing the gaming industry at the time.

First, production costs. In this example, Bungie's profit-per-sale would have been much higher if not for the additional costs of packaging, shipping, and sales agreements with retailers. Second, the difficulty of consumption. Consumers were forced to actively seek out the products they desired, whether through an online portal or a traditional brick-and-mortar store. Third, security. Developers faced constant adaptation by game-pirates attempting to find a way around paying for goods. Physical sale of these goods made it more difficult for developers to protect their products. Indeed, direct access for consumers might have led to lower overhead costs. The surplus could have been utilized for a more robust content protection system for developer's games.

Enter online payment processing. Shifting payment processing from physical to virtual attempts to solve these problems and creates a broader stream of revenue for developers. Although online payment processing comes with additional regulatory, legal, and economic hurdles, many developers have opted to follow this model for enhanced security, additional revenue, and longevity of their game. By forcing consumers to purchase their goods online, developers lower production costs, make it

---

[1] Bruce Evriss, *Game Piracy*, BRUCE ON GAMES (Apr. 23, 2008), https://www.bruceongames.com/2008/04/23/game-piracy/.

easier for consumers to purchase their goods (and therefore more likely that they will),[2] and create a more robust paper trail to help discourage piracy.

League of Legends, a game produced by Riot Games, earned $624 million in revenue from its online transactions in 2013.[3] In 2015 alone, digital gaming sales hit a record $61 billion.[4] In-game transactions make up more than three-quarters of U.S. app store revenues.[5] There is little doubt that the future of the videogame industry is through in-game purchases. Users are quick to shell out money for game additions if properly incentivized.[6] Developers will soon be scrambling to implement in-game items, which users can quickly purchase and use. The virtual market itself is booming, but this boom is not without legal and practical considerations. To successfully counter security issues while implementing such a system, many factors need to be considered. There is no consensus on how to combat certain fraud in the virtual world. In order to have successful in-game purchasing, however, some preventative measures must be in place.

---

[2] Laura Stevens, *Survey Shows Rapid Growth in Online Shopping*, THE WALL STREET J. (June 8, 2016, 12:03 AM), https://www.wsj.com/articles/survey-shows-rapid-growth-in-online-shopping-1465358582; Dean Takashi, *Worldwide game industry hits $91 billion in revenues in 2016, with mobile the clear leader*, VENTUREBEAT (Dec. 21, 2016, 7:00 AM), https://venturebeat.com/2016/12/21/worldwide-game-industry-hits-91-billion-in-revenues-in-2016-with-mobile-the-clear-leader/.

[3] Jeff Grubb, *10 Online PC Games that Made More than $100M in Microtransaction Sales Last Year*, VENTUREBEAT (Jan. 20, 2014 10:30 AM), https://venturebeat.com/2014/01/20/10-online-pc-games-that-made-more-than-100m-in-microtransaction-sales-last-year/.

[4] Tom DiChristopher, *Digital Gaming Sales Hit Record $61B: Report*, CNBC (Jan. 26, 2016, 10:03 AM), https://www.cnbc.com/2016/01/26/digital-gaming-sales-hit-record-61-billion-in-2015-report.html.

[5] *Id.* (The top three are (i) digital gaming with $61B, (ii) PC-based gaming with $32B, and (iii) Tablet/Smartphone titles with $25B.)

[6] Maggie Nazarenus, *Tips to Monetizing a Mobile Game in China*, TECHINASIA (Oct. 22, 2015), https://www.techinasia.com/talk/tips-monetizing-mobile-game-china.

The in-game purchasing model will, in all likelihood, continue to grow.[7] This growth presents lucrative business opportunities for developers, as well as an increased risk of fraud and other deception by criminals. To take advantage of the former without the latter hurting a developer's business or customers, careful steps must be taken at two stages: the implementation stage and the contractual stage. At the implementation stage, developers will have to implement fraud-detection services and design ironclad systems to fight against virtual crime, while still providing an enjoyable user experience. During the contractual stage, developers will have to navigate the tricky waters of electronic payments with banks, payment systems, and their consumers. Both involve serious legal and practical considerations and, without proper planning, can spell disaster for a developer.

In using more modern payment systems, developers are faced with new risks, legal and practical, that they will have to consider. They must balance user-facing systems with payment systems concerns, with the developer's needs caught in the middle. This paper examines the various hurdles developers will have to overcome in implementing their online payment system, including the expected issues and ways to mitigate some of those risks. In addition to payment processing, some agreements with third parties are necessary. First, an internet merchant account or alternative payment option to give developers the authority to perform online transactions. Second, a payment system consisting of a payment processor and payment gateway is needed in order to process the payment information and pass that information to the bank. This paper will examine those agreements, as well as agreements between the merchant and the consumer.

a. Background: Electronic Payment Processing

Understanding how electronic payment systems function requires a preliminary understanding of the types of transactions that take place within

[7] Brian Sinclair, *Console Microtransactions: $352 Million Annually and Growing*, GamesIndustry.biz (Mar. 26, 2014), http://www.gamesindustry.biz/articles/2014-03-26-console-microtransactions-USD352-million-annually-and-growing.

the virtual sphere.[8] Goods exchanged online generally fall into two categories: consumable or non-consumable goods.

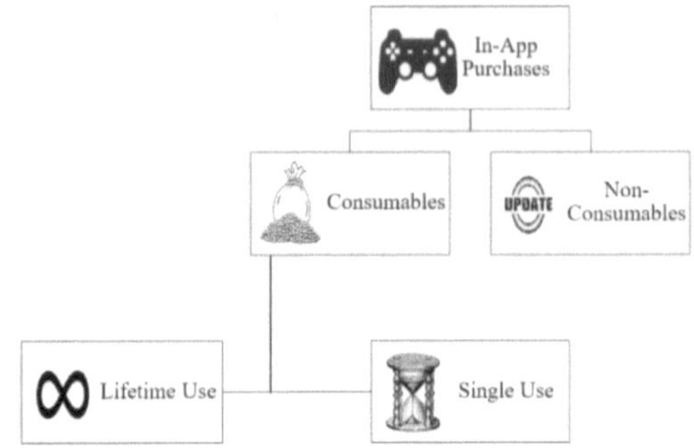

Figure 1. Types of In-App Purchases

Consumable goods refer to items that the developer wants the consumer to use over time. These include items that the consumer's in-game character uses to improve their character (e.g., clothing additions, weapon attachments, etc.) and those they can replenish eventually, such as tokens to purchase premium items. Non-consumable goods are items that last forever, such as premium versions of the game, the elimination of ads, or extra content.[9] For the most part, these present similar legal and practical considerations, although consumable goods might require a higher level of protection against fraud and abuse due to their fungible nature.

II. Existing Models for In-Game Currency

Before developers can begin selling items, add-ons, or other in-game content, they must decide on the type of currency that will control in their game. Three different models currently exist for establishing a

[8] Yaniv Nizan, *Consumable, Non Consumable Items and What's in Between*, SOOMLA (Mar. 12, 2013), http://blog.soom.la/2013/03/consumable-non-consumable-items-and.html; *see also, infra* Figure 1. Types of In-App Purchases.

[9] Yaniv Nizan, *Consumable, Non Consumable Items and What's in Between*, SOOMLA (Mar. 12, 2013), http://blog.soom.la/2013/03/consumable-non-consumable-items-and.html.

payment-system in-game: the no in-game currency model, the single currency model, and the multiple currency model.[10]

a. The No In-Game Currency Model

Perhaps the most familiar type of in-game transaction would simply be having no in-game currency whatsoever. Developers who sell their games through an online medium are likely already familiar with this model. Wanting to sell a new weapon? Simply charge the user with a real currency for that item, mimicking online purchases for real goods.

Foregoing in-game currency in favor of real-world currency allows for effective discounting procedures and use of sales to encourage users to purchase additional items or item bundles.[11] Perhaps the most well-known example of this type of structure is the Valve's Mann Co. Online Store.[12] In Team Fortress 2, a popular online game developed by Valve, users are able to purchase various items, including certain hats for their character, spending real world money to do so. These hats are simple cosmetic changes for characters and do not add to the actual gameplay, although the tongue-in-cheek Valve description might claim differently.[13]

---

[10] *Looking at In-Game Currencies*, GAMESPARKS: BLOG, https://www.gamesparks.com/blog/looking-at-in-game-currencies/ (last visited Dec. 30, 2018).

[11] *Id.*

[12] VALVE CORP., *Mann Co. Online Store*, TEAMFORTRESS.COM, http://store.teamfortress.com/ (last visited Feb. 4, 2018).

[13] VALVE CORP., *Team Fortress 2: Classless Update*, TEAMFORTRESS.COM, http://www.teamfortress.com/classless/day01.php (last visited Feb. 4, 2018) ("Throughout history, men have worn hats as a way of showing how much better they are than other men. 'I buy hats,' a behatted man seems to say. 'I am better than you.'").

Whatever the purpose of cosmetic items within their games, the Valve cosmetic item economy was valued at around $50 million in 2010.[14] Developers can successfully implement in-game purchasing without any additional currency creation. Despite the ease of access, most developers opt for one of the other two models of in-game purchasing. While these other models are more lucrative, their use creates additional legal hurdles to be considered.

b. The Single-Currency Model

Perhaps the best-known game that uses the single currency model is Blizzard's Hearthstone, which uses gold as its in-game currency.[15] Users can obtain gold through winning games or completing activities (often in the form of "quests" or other in-game challenges), through non-gameplay-related mechanisms such as daily drops.[16] This gold allows players to purchase new items (usually in the form of semi-randomized item packs) for their game.[17] However, players also have the option of purchasing some of these items directly using real-world currency.[18] Thus, players are encouraged to exchange real-world money for virtual money to obtain certain goods they would normally have to wait for, or in some cases be virtually unable to obtain in the regular progression of the game, or use money to complete many more activities not available in the standard game.[19] Where virtual currency can be exchanged for real currency, certain

---

[14] Owen Good, *Analyst Pegs Team Fortress 2 Hat Economy at $50 Million*, KOTAKU (Dec. 17, 2011, 3:00 PM), http://kotaku.com/5869042/analyst-pegs-team-fortress-2-hat-economy-at-50-million.

[15] Daniel Friedman, *Is Hearthstone Pay-to-Win? We find out*, Polygon (May 9, 2014, 1:00 PM), https://www.polygon.com/2014/5/9/5699178/hearthstone-pay-to-win.

[16] *Id.*

[17] *Id.*

[18] *Id.*

[19] *Id.*

regulatory obligations under the Bank Secrecy Act, discussed later in this article, could apply.[20]

c. The Multiple-Currency Model

The last currency model available to developers is the multiple-currency model, which utilizes soft currency (currency that players can earn in-game relatively easily by completing tasks and levels) and hard currency (currency that, while given out by the game in some situations, is mostly reserved for players who wish to purchase it with real currency). Implementing this model triggers similar legal considerations to games that employ the single currency model

Most of the top-grossing mobile games use this model,[21] but it is less prevalent in traditional console games. Some games, such as Bungie's Destiny, utilize the multiple-currency system in unique ways, blending soft- and hard-currency together to allow players to earn each in a multitude of ways, such as earning hard currency by achieving certain milestones in-game or by dismantling certain rare items acquired through gameplay.[22] One game, Battlefront 2, temporarily suspended its multiple-currency system due to widespread player backlash.[23] Many argued that unlocking normal gameplay elements without utilizing hard currency

---

[20] U.S. Dep't of the Treas. Fin. Crimes Enf't Network [hereinafter FinCEN], FIN-2013-G001, Application of FinCEN's Regulations to Persons Administering, Exchanging, or Using Virtual Currencies (Mar. 18, 2013), https://www.fincen.gov/sites/default/files/shared/FIN-2013-G001.pdf.

[21] Zeke, *The Top Ten Highest Grossing Mobile Games (And How They Got There)*, N.Y. Film Acad. Student Res. (July 22, 2016), https://www.nyfa.edu/student-resources/the-top-ten-highest-grossing-mobile-games-and-how-they-got-there/.

[22] Edmond Tran, *Destiny 2 Guide: How Currency Works*, GameSpot (Oct. 23, 2017, 3:17 PM), https://www.gamespot.com/articles/destiny-2-guide-how-currency-works/1100-6453201/.

[23] Jethro Mullen & Ivana Kottasová, *Star Wars video game maker apologizes after uproar from fans*, CNN: Money (Nov. 17, 2017, 12:38 AM), http://money.cnn.com/2017/11/16/technology/battlefront-ii-star-wars-game-ea-costs/index.html.

would take such an exorbitant amount of time that it would put non-paying players at an unfair disadvantage.[24] However, the publisher later revealed that removing the hard currency system had caused the game to miss sales targets, and announced that it would eventually re-implement the hard currency.[25]

III. Regulatory Barriers

Deciding the type of currency model to use is only the first step in incorporating electronic purchasing into a game. Developers who choose to create their own currency could run into a litany of regulatory requirements that the Department of the Treasury demands traditional virtual currency providers to follow.[26] These guidelines were created primarily to address the rise of Bitcoin as a virtual currency,[27] but the advice is potentially applicable to regular in-game currency creation as well. Developers need to familiarize themselves with the general provisions to help avoid running into legal trouble down the line.

a. Who Must Comply?

The Federal Crimes Enforcement Network (FinCEN) is responsible for "safeguard[ing] the financial system from illicit use and combat[ting] money laundering and promot[ing] national security through the collection,

---

[24] Matt Davidson, *Someone's Estimated How Long it Takes to Unlock Everything in Star Wars: Battlefront 2 (Too Long)*, IGN US (Nov. 15, 2017, 6:53 AM), http://www.ign.com/articles/2017/11/15/someones-estimated-how-long-it-takes-to-unlock-everything-in-star-wars-battlefront-2-too-long.

[25] Samit Sakar, *Star Wars Battlefront 2 Sales Miss Targets, EA Blames Loot Crate Controversy (Update)*, POLYGON (Jan. 30, 2018, 5:05 PM), https://www.polygon.com/2018/1/30/16952396/star-wars-battlefront-2-sales-loot-boxes-returning.

[26] FINCEN, FIN-2013-G001, APPLICATION OF FINCEN'S REGULATIONS TO PERSONS ADMINISTERING, EXCHANGING, OR USING VIRTUAL CURRENCIES (Mar. 18, 2013), https://www.fincen.gov/sites/default/files/shared/FIN-2013-G001.pdf.

[27] Bitcoin, a virtual currency that exists on the blockchain, revolutionized the cryptocurrency trading market. Trading as high as $20,000 USD at times, the Department of Treasury created guidelines to help regulate the market and protect against fraud.

analysis, and dissemination of financial intelligence and strategic use of financial authorities."[28] To that end, FinCEN is responsible for regulating and monitoring major financial institutions to ensure adherence to minimum security and fraud-prevention standards. FinCEN uses the Bank Secrecy Act[29] along with various anti-money laundering provisions to regulate financial institutions.[30]

Under this Act, money transmitters are required to maintain certain records and report certain transactions to FinCEN.[31] The guidance makes it clear that users purchasing virtual currencies are not subject to the provisions of the Bank Secrecy Act, because purchasing alone does not meet the definition of money transmitter under the Act.[32] An entity engaged in the business of exchanging virtual currency for real currency, funds, or other virtual currency (an exchanger), or a person engaged in the business of issuing (putting into circulation) a virtual currency, and who has the authority to redeem (to withdraw from circulation) such virtual currency (an administrator) would be considered money transmitters if they (1) accept and transmit a convertible virtual currency or (2) buy or sell convertible virtual currency for any reason.[33] Game developers could be considered administrators under this act, while the payment processors (discussed in greater detail later) could be considered the exchangers. Additionally, for an administrator to be considered a money transmitter, he

---

[28] FinCEN, Mission, https://www.fincen.gov/about/mission (last visited Feb. 4, 2017).

[29] Bank Secrecy Act, 31 U.S.C. § 5311 et. seq. (2012); *see also* Bank Secrecy Act of 1970, Pub. L. No. 91-508, 84 Stat. 1118 (1970). Act of Oct. 26, 1970, Pub. L. No. 91-508.

[30] FinCEN, Frequently Asked Questions, https://www.fincen.gov/frequently-asked-questions (last visited Dec. 8, 2017).

[31] FinCEN, *supra* note 28 at 1.

[32] *Id.*

[33] *Id.* at 4.

must facilitate the movement of funds between different persons or locations.[34]

An important legal debate arises at this point. The guideline defines convertible virtual currency as virtual currency that (1) has an equivalent value in real currency or (2) acts as a substitute for real currency.[35] While FIN-2013-G001 was designed to regulate virtual currencies such as Bitcoin, currencies that have less real-world exchange value present a question of legitimate regulation.[36] For example, from an administrator's standpoint, a virtual world that allows its players to purchase gold or coin to purchase other user-generated cosmetic goods could fall under these regulations. Imagine that one user creates an item for consumption and sells it for virtual currency to another user. The seller then wishes to cash out his virtual currency for real-world dollars. The game developer arguably could have facilitated the movement of funds between the seller and buyer, and eventually moved the funds from an online repository to a real-world one (the seller's bank account).[37]

What about games in which the virtual economy is the end-all of the transaction? In some games, users can spend real-world currency to purchase virtual currency, but are unable to cash out their virtual currency for real-world currency later on. In this instance, FinCEN has left open whether or not these regulations apply. Again, FinCEN only targets convertible virtual currency, currency that has real-world value based on real-world currency. This suggests that only virtual currency that can be exchanged for real-world currency would be subject to the Bank Secrecy Act's regulations, although it does not directly say so. While it is possible for game developers to fall outside of the regulatory scheme, forward-looking developers should carefully structure their regime to avoid the potential issues surrounding the regulations.

---

[34] *Id.*

[35] *Id.*

[36] *Regulatory Risks of In-Game and In-App Virtual Currency,* VENABLE LLP (May 22, 2017), https://www.venable.com/regulatory-risks-of-in-game-and-in-app-virtual-currency-02-01-2017/.

[37] *Id.*

An argument exists for FinCEN to intervene in fraud cases that arise with solely in-game currency, including acts such as buying in-game currency, using a more advantageous foreign currency, and reselling the in-game item to other users.[38] The agency could argue that in-game currency has real-world value, even though no traditional exchange medium exists to convert the currency. The biggest issue developers should worry about, however, is that FinCEN could begin regulating virtual currency through additional guidelines once such currency is embraced in a more widespread manner by developers. In any sense, it would be wise for developers to protect themselves from liability at the onset, even if they believe such regulations do not, or will not, apply to them.

b. What Does Compliance Mean?

If a developer is subject to complying with FinCEN's regulations, the next step is determining how these regulations affect the development of the game. For starters, developers should refer to the Bank Secrecy Act if they believe they will be subject to these regulations.[39] The Act would likely require developers to establish effective compliance programs, establish customer due diligence and monitoring programs, keep diligent records, file reports of certain transactions, and generally develop anti-money laundering programs—all standards of Bank Secrecy Act compliance.[40] These compliance issues can be costly to a developer and could require additional overhead to run a successful game.[41]

---

[38] Yinglian Xie, *There Is Real Fraud in The Underground Market For In-Game Virtual Goods*, TECHCRUNCH (Jan. 20, 2016), https://techcrunch.com/2016/01/20/virtual-goods-real-fraud/

[39] FINCEN, *supra* note 30, at 2.

[40] OFFICE OF THE CONTROLLER OF CURRENCY, BANK SECRECY ACT (BSA), https://www.occ.treas.gov/topics/compliancebsa/bsa/index-bsa.html (last visited Apr 22, 2017).

[41] The specific compliance issues developers may face in complying with FinCEN are outside the scope of this article.

Instead, developers should attempt to shield their own liability and communicate a clear boundary between themselves and their payment processor, the bank who acts as the exchanger for virtual currencies. The exchanger will, likely be subject the Bank Secrecy Act due to her role in processing the payment, i.e. exchanging real world currency for virtual one.[42] However, recall that an administrator must be dealing with convertible virtual currency for FinCEN's regulations to apply. By avoiding these types of exchanges, developers can distance themselves from the payment processor, and take definite steps to ensure that compliance with the Bank Secrecy Act is not necessary.

c. Protection from Liability

As discussed previously, it would be easy for FinCEN to claim certain developers are subject to the Bank Secrecy Act as administrators. Developers should take affirmative steps to ensure that they are not required to comply, including adding certain language to their terms of service and user agreements.

First, developers must make it clear that the virtual currency represents a license to use certain features of a game.[43] In that sense, more currency only grants users a broader license rather than increased real-world value. Making it clear that in-game currency does not represent any property interest is a first step in backing away from currency representation. This is tricky. Although the argument can be made that "real" currency has the backing of a tangible commodity such as gold, this is no longer the case in the United States.[44] Despite this, claiming that in-game currency is a license for use versus a property interest will likely help defeat an argument that the virtual currency has real-world value when

---

[42] FINCEN, *FIN-2014-R012,* REQUEST FOR ADMINISTRATIVE RULING ON THE APPLICATION OF FINCENS REGULATIONS TO A VIRTUAL CURRENCY PAYMENT SYSTEM 1 (Oct. 27, 2014) https://www.fincen.gov/sites/default/files/administrative_ruling/FIN-2014-R012.pdf .

[43] VENABLE LLP, *supra* note 36.

[44] BOARD OF GOVERNORS OF THE FEDERAL RESERVE SYSTEM, FAQS: IS U.S. CURRENCY STILL BACKED BY GOLD?, https://www.federalreserve.gov/faqs/currency_12770.htm (last visited Apr 22, 2017).

supplemented by other language. For instance, stating clearly in the end-user license agreement or during purchases that in-game currency has no value in real currency could help developers argue that their economy is self-contained and therefore inapplicable to various regulatory regimes.[45] Likewise, alerting users to the fact that the in-game currency does not correspond to any real-world currency value could make the currency appear less like real-world currency and more like in-game data.

The ability to arbitrarily change the purchase price of the in-game currency is vital.[46] Reserving the right to change the purchase price at any time will make it clear that the currency does not depend on the value of any existing real-world currency. If the value of the virtual currency is relatable or dependent on a real-world currency, enforcers at FinCEN would likely require compliance with the Bank Secrecy Act. Again, it should be the goal of the developer to avoid compliance with this Act. Protecting himself from liability at the onset is the first step in doing this.

Lastly, having cash-out and transfer restrictions can prevent the rise of in-game or real-world trading markets.[47] These types of markets can give real-world value to your in-game currency through third-party gambling markets.[48] The response way is to prevent users from the ability to cash out or transfer their virtual currency or in-game goods in any capacity, making it clear to users that virtual currency is not traditional currency. This could be achieved through a variety of methods, such as including these restrictions in agreements with users, and banning users who violate the policy. Likewise, developers could explore legal action against third-party websites that trade in the virtual currency.

---

[45] VENABLE LLP, *supra* note 36.

[46] VENABLE LLP, *supra* note 36.

[47] VENABLE LLP, *supra* note 36.

[48] Joshua Brustein & Eben Novy-Williams, *Virtual Weapons Are Turning Teen Gamers Into Serious Gamblers*, BLOOMBERG (Apr. 16, 2016), https://www.bloomberg.com/features/2016-virtual-guns-counterstrike-gambling/.

These steps have one thing in common that developers should focus on: attempting to make in-game currency have no real-world value. Any steps a developer can take to reinforce this point could help reduce the chance for that developer to be held liable under the various controlling regulations. However, taking these steps might reduce a developer's user base or monetization options. After all, these markets for in-game currency spring up because they can be popular with users and therefore lucrative. A developer must weigh the risk of bearing the compliance costs against the possibility of loss in user-base or monetization. Perhaps a developer will find it more economically beneficial to deal with the costs associated with compliance in order to facilitate a robust in-game economy. However, attempting to avoid the costs of compliance while simultaneously attempting to function as a Money Services Business by providing these exchanges can have disastrous consequences.[49]

d. Next Steps

First, a developer must decide the type of goods to sell in-game (consumables vs. non-consumables) and the type of currency structure to use (none, single, multiple). Then, the developer must avoid falling under the Bank Secrecy Act to avoid high compliance costs. Only then is the developer ready to begin organizing payment systems and working out contracts with the various actors. The legal implications and risks associated with the contracts between each actor will be discussed in greater detail in the next section, but it helps to have a basic understanding of the relationship between the developer and the payment systems.

As illustrated by Figure 2, below, a basic transaction includes the buyer of the good (in this case, the user), working with the merchant (in this case, the developer), to complete the transaction.[50] The merchant–developer then has a transaction take place with the payment gateway, which processes the transaction through its own third-party processor and banks. More often, the latter steps are packaged together

---

[49] *FinCEN Announces First BSA Enforcement Action Against Virtual Currency Exchanger*, HUNTON & WILLIAMS: PRIVACY & INFORMATION SECURITY LAW BLOG (May 12, 2015), https://www.huntonprivacyblog.com/2015/05/12/fincen-announces-first-bsa-enforcement-action-virtual-currency-exchanger/.

[50] *Id.*

as a payment system. Merchant–developers no longer have to piece together their own system to process payments; instead they can contract with companies like PayPal to handle much of the behind the scenes transactions. This is good news in legal and regulatory-risk calculations. Contracting with one company, instead of five, can help reduce some of the liability faced by merchant–developers when things go awry. Instead, merchant–developers can focus on two agreements: the agreement with the user (often in the form of a terms of service or end-user license agreement), and the agreement with the payment system. The next section will focus on these two agreements by closely examining the flow of the dollar between these actors and determining how developers can best protect themselves from liability and risk when faced with these agreements.

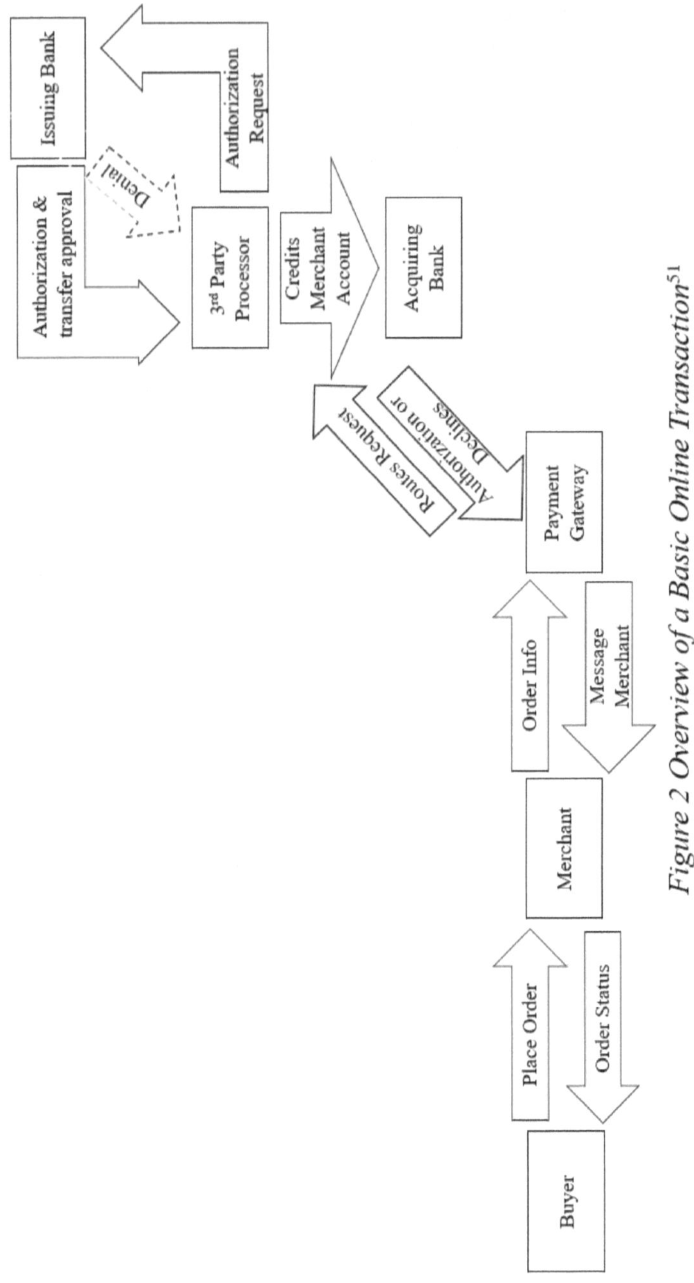

Figure 2 Overview of a Basic Online Transaction[51]

[51] *See* Lex Sheehan, *How Payment Processing Works* (1970), http://lexsheehan.blogspot.com/2013/03/how-payment-processing-works.html (last visited Apr 22, 2017).

V. CONTRACTING BETWEEN PARTIES

a. Between Developer and User

The first agreement developers should consider is the agreement with their users. Developers need to carefully consider the terms under which their game functions. In the previous sections, we discussed the FinCEN regulations and how to draft user agreements that attempt to disclaim liability. In addition to those clauses, a user agreement has to address other questions that might arise when a user purchases virtual goods. Specifically, the developer must consider the possibility of users being defrauded by third parties, protection against fraudulent transactions from users, avoiding liability for broken or unusable goods, and the potential for a data breach. The user will have questions regarding the ownership of goods in the virtual world, how to get a refund on those goods, and how to recover from a data breach. Each developer will wrestle with these questions if they want to protect themselves and cover their potential costs.

When it comes to electronic payments for virtual goods, developers should be concerned with three primary issues: fraud prevention, data breaches, and ownership of goods. In writing their terms of service or user agreements, developers should systematically attempt to deal with each of these in order to minimize the potential liability that might flow from failure to do this.

b. Preventing Fraud

First, a developer must take the necessary steps to prevent fraud. Fraud can come through a variety of avenues, including multiple account creation,[52] stolen credit card purchases and chargebacks,[53] or virtual

[52] *Fraud: Multiple Accounts/IPs*, SUPERREWARDS.COM, http://docs.superrewards.com/docs/fraud-multiple-accountsips (last visited Feb. 4, 2018).

[53] *Strategies to Protect Your Gamers and Your Revenue* 1, 3, CHASE PAYMENTECH SOLUTIONS, https://www.chasepaymentech.com/documents/safetech_bp_gaming.pdf (last visited Apr 22, 2017).

economy scams.[54] Prevention of each of these requires affirmative steps by the developer. The agreement between the user and the developer will be telling, but not enough. Take multiple account creation: A user might create multiple accounts in order to complete certain tasks more quickly, obtain consumable items that can be traded to their other accounts, or boost their character stats. This behavior can imbalance a game and put other players at an unfair disadvantage. To combat this, a developer might put a clause in the user agreement banning the use of multiple accounts. While reasonable, this is not very practical. Without actively preventing a user from creating multiple accounts, the developer is still susceptible to fraud and, therefore, additional cost that could be avoided at the onset. One potential way to avoid this cost is email verification.[55] This way, users wishing to create multiple accounts will be limited by the number of email addresses to which they have access. This is not a perfect way to prevent fraud since users are able to create email addresses using free services without any real limits. However, setting up a system in which a scammer must create both a new email address and a new account might help reduce the number of potential users committing fraud by increasing the time cost of such activity. Reducing this type of fraud benefits the developer by assuring that certain in-game items retain their value and are not nefariously created.[56]

Another type of fraud that can be prevented in development comes in the form of stolen credit cards or chargebacks. Again, developers will not be able to prevent this type of fraud simply by protecting themselves in the user agreement. To prevent the use of stolen credit cards to pay for games or in-game items, developers should take steps to verify customers' payment methods. Discussed later, with their agreements with payment systems, developers need to ensure that the payment gateway they chose to use verifies the credit card payment in certain ways. Failure to do so will result in potential liability for themselves. With regard to chargebacks,

---

[54] Kevin Sullivan, *Virtual Money Laundering and Fraud*, BANKINFORMATIONSECURITY.COM (Apr. 3, 2008), http://www.bankinfosecurity.com/virtual-money-laundering-fraud-a-809.

[55] CHASE PAYMENTECH SOLUTIONS, *supra* note 53 at 2.

[56] If, for example, a player received a certain item for creating their account, a user could create multiple accounts in order to boost their main characters attributes using that special item—decreasing the in-game value of that item.

when the credit card provider cancels a pending transaction due to error or fraud, developers must be willing to work with users. Many chargebacks happen when children buy goods with a parent's credit card.[57] This mistake can be mitigated if developers work closely with their users when these mistakes happen. For instance, an email help account operated by the developers could allow users to report and developers to detect improper transactions before they are processed. Additionally, clearly identifying the source of charges on users' credit card statements is another way developers can avoid chargebacks. Chargeback rates tend to be higher when companies attempt to anonymize their information on a consumer's bill. [58] Again, this type of fraud is better addressed in agreements between the developer and the payment gateway, but ensuring that users are aware of the steps developers are taking in the background could greatly reduce the potential for fraud.

c. Ownership of Goods

Lastly, developers should concern themselves with the ownership of virtual goods. This is where the user agreement and terms of service will come into play, communicating the ownership of the goods that the user purchases can avoid liability further down the road. Developers should communicate three things with regard to the virtual goods purchased in their game: that the goods represent a limited, nontransferable, revocable license to access certain portions of the game; a clearly stated refund policy; and that the developer maintains full control of the virtual goods with the ability to change or revoke the goods at any time.[59]

Developers are in a unique position that other sellers of property are not in. Since virtual goods are made up entirely of code, developers maintain a unique position of ownership after they have sold the goods. In a normal buyer–seller relationship, the seller's relationship with the goods

---

[57] CHASE PAYMENTECH SOLUTIONS, *supra* note 53 at 3.

[58] *Id.*

[59] *See, e.g.*, *Terms of Service: Virtual Money and Virtual Goods* (Oct. 22, 2015), NIANTIC, INC., https://www.ingress.com/terms.

ends after he has sold the goods to the buyer. The buyer is fully responsible and able to control the goods, regardless of what the seller decides later on. This is not the case with virtual goods. Once the developer has sold a virtual good to the user, the developer is still able to completely revoke or change the virtual good, either deliberately or by malfunction of the game. However, this does not mean the items are without value. Users spent an estimated $7.3 billion dollars on virtual goods alone in 2010,[60] with that number almost certainly increasing in later years. Users want their virtual goods to be considered property because of their value. Developers want to avoid this outcome at all costs; virtual goods being considered property means they have to pay out when that property is compromised in some way.

The first way in avoiding this liability is to sell the virtual good as a license and not as a good. The license will allow the user to access extra content within the game, but will not represent any real property. In this way, developers are selling software and access to the software, not actual goods. Many developers already take this route,[61] which demonstrates that this can be considered a reliable the first step in ensuring protection for the developer.

The next step, although small, is determining whether to offer refunds for the virtual goods. Doing so could, unfortunately, make the goods appear less like a license and more like traditional goods. However, offering refunds also instills a sense of security in the users. Regardless of what developers choose to do, the policies should be clearly communicated in the user agreements under the virtual goods section.

Lastly, and perhaps most importantly, is the concept of control. Developers should maintain full control over a user's virtual goods and communicate this control to avoid future liability.[62] If a developer

---

[60] Ted Sorum, *The Year In Virtual Goods By The Numbers*, TECHCRUNCH (Dec, 31, 2010), https://techcrunch.com/2010/12/31/the-year-in-virtual-goods-by-the-numbers/.

[61] Oliver Herzfeld, *What Is The Legal Status Of Virtual Goods?*, FORBES (Dec. 12, 2012, 1:09 PM), https://www.forbes.com/sites/oliverherzfeld/2012/12/04/what-is-the-legal-status-of-virtualgoods/#7f595dff108a.

[62] *Virtual Goods—Developing and Protecting a Business Model* 1-2, PILLSBURY WINTHROP SHAW PITTMAN LLP (Feb. 8, 2018),

maintains that the virtual goods represent a non-transferable license, the aspect of control should be easy to meet. A 2010 decision out of the 9th Circuit held that non-transferable licenses could not be transferred in this aspect,[63] supporting the conclusion that a developer can sell the virtual good as a license that cannot be transferred. How far a developer wishes to go in order to prevent transfer or sale of the virtual good is a business decision, but at least some restrictions must be in place to protect the developer's interest. Developers have a legitimate interest in balancing gameplay for their users, and virtual goods that are too powerful might require balance from the developer's standpoint. Maintaining this sort of control over virtual items is vital for ultimate enjoyment of the game. One author has pointed out that this sort of balancing might be considered a "taking" by the court.[57] Developers should take the aforementioned steps in order to maintain control over the virtual items.

d. Data Breaches

Next, developers need to think about their liability if a user's data is compromised. When a user conducts a transaction, the transaction falls into one of two categories. The first, card-present transactions, occur when the user and the card are physically present.[64] Credit card providers claim that this is a more secure transaction and that the assignment of liability reflects this security.[65] Regardless of the technology used (chip reader or magnetic slide reader), the merchant is typically[66] not liable for fraudulent

---

https://www.pillsburylaw.com/images/content/1/0/v2/102373/FACTSHEETVirtualGoods.pdf.

[63] Vernor v. Autodesk, Inc., 621 F.3d 1102, 1111 (9th Cir. 2010).

[64] Phillip Parker, *Card Present Definition,* CARDPAYMENTOPTIONS.COM, https://www.cardpaymentoptions.com/glossary/card-present-definition/ (last visited Apr. 22, 2017).

[65] *EMV Chip Liability Shift: Why it pays to adopt new technology* 1, VISA, https://www.visa.com/chip/merchants/grow-your-business/payment-technologies/credit-card-chip/docs/VISA_LIABILITY_SHIFT_FINAL.pdf (Last visited Nov. 19, 2017).

[66] Some might argue that chipped cards force liability on the merchant since the card issuer recommends a certain security measure and the merchant chooses whether or not to

transactions because the payment system can verify the legitimacy of the card through its terminals, and the merchant can verify the physical presence of the user.[67] Unfortunately, this type of transaction does not describe the typical virtual good purchase: card-not-present transactions, the type of transactions that typically occur online through websites. Game developers cannot verify the physical presence of the customer and the payment system cannot verify the legitimacy of the card through traditional means. As a result, the liability for fraudulent payments shifts from the issuer to the merchant.[68] Not all hope is lost for developers, however. Issuers are moving toward taking on this liability to help mitigate the costs of issuing new credit cards for users who are victims of fraud and restore faith in the ecommerce market.[69] If issuers begin to assume this liability, developers might find themselves in a better position. Until then, however, developers must find ways to protect user data and reduce fraud.

There are several techniques to achieve these goals through agreements with the payment system. Additionally, there are a few forward-facing steps developers can take with their user agreements to help prevent the liability at this stage. First, developers should take affirmative steps with their users to verify user data. One way to do this is through data retention. Communicating to the user how their data is stored can help a developer alleviate the concerns users might have with handing over their data. Data retention can help law enforcement track down fraudsters, help the developer respond to breaches, and potentially track down fraudsters to recover the goods or funds in question. The drawback of this approach is the necessity to have a more robust data-security service and proper safeguards when dealing with user data. Using tools like encryption, data

---

comply. For the purposes of this paper, this is irrelevant. The security is still theoretically higher than in card-not-present transactions.

[67] Card issuers likely feel comfortable with taking on liability here because they know there had to be a physical card, and that card created a transaction trail.

[68] *Card-Not-Present Fraud: A Primer on Trends and Authentication Process* 14, SMART CARD ALL. PAYMENTS COUNCIL (Feb. 2014), http://www.emv-connection.com/downloads/2014/01/CNP-WP-012414.pdf; *Why are e-Commerce Merchants Liable for Fraud?*, VERIFI, http://www.verifi.com/kb/why-are-e-commerce-merchants-liable-for-fraud/ (last visited Feb. 4, 2018).

[69] *Id.*

retention policies, and in-house fraud-prevention services, developers can secure the confidence of their users and help reduce the potential for breaches to occur. Developers' user agreements should communicate any data retention, encryption, validation, or other security-related policies to users and force them to agree to the terms. Communicating these policies might help developers disclaim liability if there is a breach.

Taking these steps could help developers increase the value of their online economy. With greater transaction security, users feel more confident buying items and spending real-world money.[70] When users are prevented from fraudulently acquiring virtual goods, those goods could be considered more valuable in-game and can generate more revenue for the developer.

i. Push-Back From Users

It is important to note here the role of the user in all of this. Up to this point, this article has assumed that developers are creating the virtual goods in question. As virtual worlds become more sophisticated, developers can find themselves faced with users creating virtual goods—such as costumes or housing for digital avatars—to sell in-game.[71] As a result, users are becoming more willing to fight against the ownership of the goods belonging to the developer. These virtual goods, which in some ways resemble user-generated intellectual property, can be important to users. Users' desire to protect their own creations will likely increase. There is at least one case in which a user took out a mortgage on his house to purchase in-game content.[72] Users would likely be disappointed if they

---

[70] Milam Aiken & Mahesh Vanjani, *Likelihood of Purchase On-line: Reliability, Security, and Design*, 4.2 COMMUNICATIONS OF THE INT'L INFO. MGMT. ASS'N. 1, 7 (2004).

[71] Benjamin Tarsa, *Licensing of Virtual Goods: Misconceptions of Ownership* para. 31, GNOVIS (Apr. 26, 2012), http://www.gnovisjournal.org/2012/04/26/licensing-of-virtual-goods-misconceptions-of-ownership/.

[72] Oliver Chiang, *Meet The Man Who Just Made A Half Million From The Sale Of Virtual Property*, FORBES (Nov. 23, 2010, 7:20PM), https://www.forbes.com/sites/oliverchiang/2010/11/13/meet-the-man-who-just-made-a-cool-half-million-from-the-sale-of-virtual-property/#7c44ca2e21cd.

found out there was no ownership conferred in that purchase. In order to prevent the stifling of innovation, developers need to find ways to work with these users to protect their own interests while still allowing user-generated virtual goods.

One example we see of this phenomenon is *Evans v. Linden Research, Inc.*[73] In *Evans*, plaintiffs were suing the developer of Second Life, a game in which players can create characters called avatars to represent themselves and interact with other avatars in a huge virtual world. Users can buy and sell items, create homes, and buy virtual land from the developer.[74] In this case, users purchased items from the developer and, soon thereafter, their accounts were suspended for unrelated reasons.[75] The users brought suit against the developer, claiming that their virtual goods had real-world value and that they weren't compensated for that value.[76] The case ultimately settled, with the developer having to pay out to the users for their lost value.[77]

Second Life is one virtual world in which user-created goods are important. Although this case is now several years old, it represents the dilemma that developers face regarding virtual goods. The developers of Second Life have an interest in both ensuring that ownership of the goods remains in their hands, while also encouraging innovation among players to create unique, valuable goods. This dilemma will continue to evolve, and the solution is not entirely clear. One frequently discussed solution is the separation user-generated goods from non-user-generated goods, allowing users to own their virtual goods in-game as personal property, while maintaining the license structure for non-user-generated goods.[78] Another

---

[73] Evans v. Linden Research, Inc., No. C 11-01078 DMR, 2012 U.S. Dist. LEXIS 166006 (N.D. Cal. Nov. 20, 2012).

[74] *Id.* at *2.

[75] *Id.* at *3.

[76] *Id.* at *3.

[77] Evans v. Linden Research, Inc., No. C 11-01078 DMR, 2012 U.S. Dist. LEXIS 59432 *1 (N.D. Cal. Apr. 29, 2014).

[78] Kenneth Eng, *Content Creators, Virtual Goods: Who Owns Virtual Property*, 34 CARDOZO ARTS & ENT. L. J. 249, 276–77 (Apr. 19, 2016).

potential solution is granting limited property rights for user-generated content to users through the terms-of-service agreement, potentially making games more valuable.[79]

Developers must walk a fine line. The reality is that users can create real, meaningful, virtual goods that are more akin to intellectual property rights than traditional real property. Courts may be willing to accept an expansive view of the traditional model of developer-owned virtual goods. As a result, developers should consider getting ahead of the curve by granting very limited property rights to their users to keep up with the changing landscape.

e. Between the Developer and the Payment System

So far, we have only discussed agreements between the developer and the user at length. Now we move to agreements between developers and payment systems. These agreements are mostly out of the developers' hands, though developers still have a responsibility to ensure that their agreements with payment systems do not conflict with user terms-of-service agreements. Although they are less able to modify their agreements with payment systems, developers should closely examine the agreement to guarantee the best contract possible. There are key contractual provisions developers should scrutinize. First, developers should inspect the liability of the payment system in the result of a data breach. Second, they should examine the fee and price point using an interchange table. Third, developers should review the indemnification clause in the agreement between the parties.

i. Data Breaches

The first item developers should look for is the protections that the payment system offers for liability in the result of data breaches. There are three main areas to inspect here: the liability of the payment system if a data breach occurs, the storage of customer data, and the prevention of fraud. The developer is typically held responsible in "card-not-present"

---

[79] Leah Shen, *Who Owns the Virtual Items?*, 11 DUKE L. & TECH. 1, 29 (2010).

transactions.[80] Payment systems have started to consider bearing the liability for these transactions. The developer should examine the contract to see how much liability the payment system is prepared to accept. If none, which is likely the case at the moment, developers should be concerned with how their users' data is stored and used in a typical transaction. If a user's data is compromised, the user will look first to the developer for recovery. While the developer may not bear responsibility if the breach was the fault of the payment system, examining the contract with the payment system might help avoid future problems.

To protect user data, developers should consider features such as the use of a Chip Authentication Program (CPA)/Dynamic Passcode Authentication (DPA), 3D secure, and tokenization.[81] MasterCard and Visa employ CPA/DPA, respectively. These systems work similarly to an EMV chip; when a transaction is processed a record of that transaction is created through a readable cryptogram unique to the user. This program was released in Sweden and the UK with limited success, though it was used primarily by financial institutions rather than consumers.[82] A more popular data-security method is 3D Secure, which is a program originally deployed by Visa[83] that verifies users' information through a database shared by major card providers and helps eliminate some of the anonymity from card-not-present transactions.[84] Tokenization replaces the user's payment with a token that is provided by the issuer, and requested at the time of purchase. Tokenization is considered particularly secure because it substitutes secure data during the transaction with data that has no exploitable value.[85]

---

[80] SMART CARD ALL. PAYMENTS COUNCIL, *supra* note 68, at 15.

[81] SMART CARD ALL. PAYMENTS COUNCIL, *supra* note 68 at 16.

[82] SMART CARD ALL. PAYMENTS COUNCIL, *supra* note 68 at 16.

[83] John T. Mulqueen, Visa USA tightens security with Arcot, ZDNet (May 16, 2001, 3:30AM), http://www.zdnet.com/article/visa-usa-tightens-security-with-arcot/.

[84] SMART CARD ALL. PAYMENTS COUNCIL, *supra* note 68 at 16; *D Secure*, SECUREPAY, https://www.securepay.com.au/developers/products-andservices/3d-secure/ (last visited Apr 23, 2017).

[85] SMART CARD ALL. PAYMENTS COUNCIL, *supra* note 68 at 17.

Deciding which payment system to use could depend largely on a developer's commitment to preventing data breaches. Although the developer will likely be held responsible for any data breaches in the current market, movement toward issuer liability might start emerging over the next few years. Developers should carefully consider how much risk they are comfortable accepting and carefully research the company with which they are contracting.

ii. Fees and Price Point

One area without much room for negotiation is fees. Each payment system will likely charge some fee as a result of processing the transaction, as well as a backend charge of processing the transaction by the payment processor, discussed in what is called an interchange table.[86] The interchange table refers to the fee that backend processors takes as their cut of the transaction. This, coupled with the fee that the payment system charges, can spell trouble for a developer. Major payment processors typically charge customers a percentage of the transaction, plus a fixed amount. Both of these figures can vary based on the customer's agreement with the payment processors and the details of the transaction—including location and transaction total, among others.[87]

One major problem in implementing virtual goods is the micro-transaction model common in video games.[88] Some developers offer in-game virtual goods with narrow profit margins that can be eaten away by processing fees. Many retailers impose a minimum charge for credit card

[86] *Visa USA Interchange Reimbursement Fees* 1, VISA (Oct. 14, 2017), https://usa.visa.com/dam/VCOM/global/support-legal/documents/visa-usa-interchange-reimbursement-fees.pdf.

[87] *See, e.g. id.*; *Pricing*, BRAINTREE PAYMENTS, https://www.braintreepayments.com/braintree-pricing (last visited February 4, 2018); *PayPal Merchant Fees: Current Rates for all Merchant Accounts,* PAYPAL US (March 29, 2017), https://www.paypal.com/us/webapps/mpp/merchant-fees.

[88] Brian Crecente, *What Are DLC, Loot Boxes and Microtransactions? An Explainer,* ROLLING STONE: GLIXEL (Nov. 28, 2017), https://www.rollingstone.com/glixel/features/dlc-loot-boxes-microtransactions-prize-crates-explained-w512762.

transactions to address this same issue: Stores lose money based on interchange fees and processing a credit card transaction under a certain amount can erode, or even eliminate, their profits on small transactions.[89] While virtual goods do not face the same production costs as real-world goods, developers should still be aware of the risk of losing out on smaller transaction. For this reason, a developer might choose to process payments through a micro-transaction payment processor. Not all payment systems offer this service,[90] but some allow the bundling of micro-payments together and processing them as a single, larger transaction. The drawback to this is that providers sometimes charge larger fees to process micro-transaction bundles. A savvy developer might use one payment system for large transactions and another for micro-transactions.[91] Whatever route developers choose, they should carefully examine the agreements to obtain the best fee arrangement for their particular business plans. Since developers are likely to offer both lower-cost virtual goods that are considered micro-transactions and high-cost goods that are not, they should try to find a payment system that can handle both at a price that meets their needs.

iii. Indemnification

Another factor that developers should consider in payment agreements is indemnification. In an indemnification clause, one party (the indemnifier) agrees to hold harmless and defends another (the indemnified) against third-party claims caused by the indemnifiers actions. In standard indemnification agreements, the payment processor indemnifies the customer against suits caused by its malfeasance.[92] Nothing special needs

---

[89] Kristy Welsh, *Why Do Some Stores Have Credit Card Minimums?*, CREDITREPAIR.COM: BLOG, https://www.creditrepair.com/blog/finance/why-do-some-stores-have-credit-card-minimums/ (last visited Feb. 4, 2018).

[90] *Does Stripe support microtransactions and will my fees be the same?*, STRIPE: SUPPORT, https://support.stripe.com/questions/does-stripe-support-microtransactions-and-will-my-fees-be-the-same (last visited Apr 23, 2017).

[91] Sys. & Method for processing microtransactions, U.S. Patent No. 8,429,072 B1 (filed Sep 27, 2011).

[92] *See, e.g.*, *Authorize.net Payment Gateway Merchant Service Agreement* 4, AUTHORIZE.NET, https://www.authorize.net/content/dam/authorize/documents/CyberSource_Service_Agreement_UK.pdf (last visited Apr 23, 2017).

to be added to traditional indemnification clauses, but developers will want to guarantee that they are protected against suits prompted by the processor's actions. This is especially important when it comes to data breaches. When users discover that their data has been breached, they will likely come after the developer, even if the developer is not at fault. Here, if a suit moves forward, an indemnification clause will ensure that the developer is held harmless and defended by the payment processor for the processor's mistakes. An indemnification agreement should suffice, but it is important for developers to conduct due diligence to prevent surprises from happening later. There likely is not much room for negotiation in this area, but most major payment systems should have some sort of indemnification clause in their agreements, so it is not something a developer should spend too much time worrying about so long as they are indemnified from third-party claims arising from data breaches.

V. CONCLUSION

When considering payment systems in a video game, developers are faced with various legal, regulatory, and practical considerations. This article serves as a primer to the types of issues developers should evaluate, including their agreements with their users and payment processors. Developers need to be certain that they are compliant with applicable financial regulations, including careful steps to shift liability away from them. Complex issues arise regarding the flow of the dollar from the user to the developer's pockets, data breaches, ownership of the goods, and fraud prevention. To have an in-game virtual goods system, steps need to be taken to protect developers against liability.

Bungie made it simple to share Halo 2's Multiplayer Map Pack, but developers and users have come a long way since the release of that game. Now, users are demanding more property interests over their in-game goods, and developers are grappling with how to respond to these demands. Developers must shift the risk of liability and protect themselves through the terms of service and other agreements made with parties involved in the processing of electronic payments. The coming years will likely see stricter regulation of virtual currency, greater judicial crackdowns on virtual goods ownership, and increased liability on the card issuer for fraud. Despite these changes, developers should prepare for the changing landscape while drafting agreements that protect them in the current environment and those to come.

www.ingramcontent.com/pod-product-compliance
Lightning Source LLC
Chambersburg PA
CBHW030741180526
45163CB00003B/871